Savour the seasons

By

Pat Hughes
and
Eleanor Cameron

Published by
The Kitchener-Waterloo Record
1993

Canadian Cataloguing in Publication Data

Hughes, Pat

Savour the Seasons

Includes index.
ISBN 0-9697653-0-4

1. Cookery. 2. Menus. I. Cameron, Eleanor
II. Kitchener-Waterloo Record III. Title.

TX715.6.H825 1993 641.5 C93-090651-9

Cover and illustrations: Diane Shantz
Editing: Kathryn Storring
Printing: Cober Printing, Kitchener, Ontario

For additional copies of Savour the Seasons contact:

The Kitchener-Waterloo Record,
225 Fairway Rd S.,
Kitchener, Ont., N2G 4E5
Telephone: (519) 894-2231

Contents

Acknowledgements

It would be impossible to write a cookbook, even one that is a collection of previously published recipes, without a great deal of encouragement and help.

Our families deserve special recognition: they patiently taste-tested all of the recipes here, plus those that didn't meet our standards. In the process, they have become very good, constructive critics. Thank you, Doug, Steve, Margaret and Lindsey.
Thanks also goes to our extended families, friends and neighbors. Our readers as well as the students from our cooking classes, which included everything from barbecuing to microwave cooking, also deserve credit; their feedback helped to keep us alert and aware of their interests and concerns.

A special thank you goes to those readers, friends and relatives who shared and exchanged recipes with us over the years; some of these are recognized in the recipe names.

Several employees of the Kitchener-Waterloo Record (past and present) have shared their expertise and provided encouragement. Frances Denney and Wayne MacDonald were the first to have sufficient faith to hire us in 1978; many others since then, especially our current editor Carol Jankowski and community relations manager Owen Lackenbauer, have been tremendously supportive. Thanks also go to newspaper editors in Stratford, Peterborough, Brantford and New Hamburg, and at Highlights and Leisure World magazines.

Preparing a manuscript for publication required help with typing, editing and proof-reading; for that we thank Wendi Hiebert, Jonathan Alberts, Janet Baxter and Jean Lawless.

Last, but not least, thank you to our Moms; these two good cooks first sparked our interest in good food.

Introduction

This book represents the achievement of a long-term goal — the publication in book form of a compilation of our favorite "tried and true" recipes.

Each recipe has been personally tested by one of us, and has been specifically chosen from our previously published newspaper columns:

- **In Good Taste** (Kitchener-Waterloo Record)
- **Plain and Fancy** (Stratford Beacon Herald)
- **Tasty Topics** (Peterborough Examiner)
- **Mastering Microwaves** (Brantford Expositor)
- or from special feature articles written for **Highlights** and **Leisure World** magazines.

Our readers have been requesting a cookbook since the column was first published in 1978, when home economists Pat Hughes, Marie Hunt and Ruth Rae wrote under the "nom de plume" of Miranda Martin. Marie and Ruth left in 1980. Until her untimely death in 1984, Gwen Simpson worked with Pat.

Eleanor Cameron joined Pat in 1984 to continue as a team, writing the daily column to the present. Although a few recipes date from the early years, most of the recipes included in this book are from the past nine years.

Each of the above women, all professional home economists, influenced the format and quality of the columns, and ultimately this book.

As well, each recipe is a reflection of the authors' training, with particular attention paid to cost, nutrition, time and ease of preparation, clarity of instruction and versatility — with good taste always being the dominant factor.

Although times change, good taste and fine food are timeless. In keeping with the lifestyle of the '90s, this book of menus and recipes proves again that home eating and home entertainment are not only economical and nutritious, but the best investment in

Introduction continued

quality living. Both nourish the body and the soul!

In response to our readers, we have chosen a menu format for the book. They tell us that they appreciate suggestions on "what to serve with what." Thus, the menus illustrate which foods complement each other, and how a specific recipe best becomes part of a meal. We recognize that menus planned by us will not always be what you want to serve on any given day. So we encourage you to experiment and make changes to meet your needs and taste preferences.

It is our hope that the principles of fine cooking translate into the pleasures of fine eating and dining.

BON APPETIT!

Pat Hughes and
Eleanor Cameron

Postscript: Eleanor and I "talked" cookbook for several years. In the spring of 1991, as soon as Eleanor's final exams for her degree in applied arts were over, we started putting our ideas and thoughts on paper. Then she learned that she had cancer.
Between two major surgeries, chemotherapy and radiation treatments and a broken arm, we worked together, planning formats and menus and selecting recipes for the book. It is truly a 50-50 collaboration.
Eleanor lived to see the manuscript completed and handed over to our publisher; she did not live to see the book you hold in your hands.
It was my privilege to have known and worked with this warm, intelligent and very spunky woman. Her too early death is a great loss to her family and friends, to the community and to our profession.

\- Pat

Seasonal Menus

Spring is in the air

Just one day of balmy weather is all it takes to give us a feeling of relief and hope. Even if the weather reverts to winter, we know that there are brighter, warmer days ahead.

During this transitional season, we progress, with the sun, from snow banks to snow drops, from brown lawns to green, from snow boots to sandals, and from hearty winter meals to rhubarb, asparagus and barbecues.

The longer hours of daylight, the warmer sunshine and the heightened colors of nature are truly a tonic.

A taste of the Emerald Isle

6 servings

On St. Patrick's Day, we need a meal to make those Irish eyes smile — tasty, but not pretentious.

An Irish meal, as we know it here, might include corned beef and cabbage, certainly potatoes, soda bread and Irish coffee. Lamb stew or boiled bacon or ham served with colcannon, plain soda bread and Guinness or Irish whisky is probably more authentic. We have compromised, in typical Canadian fashion, with the following menu.

Health and long life to you, and may your bones rest in Ireland.

Braised Lamb Shanks, ***Page 109***
Colcannon, ***Page 139***
Irish Soda Bread, ***Page 198***
Emerald Isle Salad, ***Page 83***
Irish Coffee Pie, ***Page 181***

Welcome spring

2 - 4 servings

We think the astrological calendar has the right idea — the year should begin on March 21. Spring is a time of new growth and new babies for nature's wild creatures.

Spring can be a tease, with mild, sunny days followed by cold rain — even snow! — but we do celebrate its arrival.

Whether spring makes you think of a new wardrobe, spring-cleaning, gardening or planning a vacation, it brings an emotional and physical "lift".

Fresh Asparagus Bisque, ***Page 68***
Honey-Lemon Glazed Turkey Wings, ***Page 126***
Potatoes
Carrot-Waldorf Salad, ***Page 81***
Baked Orange Flans, ***Page 167***

Choose an Easter dinner to match the day

The date of Easter is determined by the moon and it can be as early as March 21 or as late as April 25. Because spring weather is notoriously unpredictable, a March Easter may be balmy and an April Easter wintry.

We planned two Easter menus assuming that you will want a hearty meal for an early Easter, and lighter, springtime fare for a late Easter.

But be prepared to reverse the two, or select your favorite foods from either menu for an in-between kind of day.

Early Easter

8 servings

Mushroom Tarts, *Page36*
AND/OR
Salsa Aspic Ring With Crab Meat Dip, *Page 46*
Dressed Pork Tenderloins, *Page 102*
OR
Cider Baked Ham, *Page 105*
Sunny Carrots and Leeks Casserole, *Page 147*
Audrey's Salad, *Page 73*
Apple Cheesecake Viennoise, *Page 162*

Late Easter

4 - 5 servings

Soupa Avgolemono, *Page 70*
Lamb Chops With Apple-Mint Sauce, *Page 110*
Savory Potato Wedges, *Page 141*
Steamed Fresh Asparagus OR Carrot Coins
OR
Hot Herbed Tomatoes, *Page 145*
Simon's Spinach Salad With Maple Dressing, *Page 88*
Angel Cream Pavlova, *Page 179*

April Fool's Day supper

6 - 8 servings

How many times were you caught in a practical joke or sent on a "fool's errand" on April 1? We all seem to be a little silly on the first day of April; maybe an impromptu supper would be a good way to cap the day.

For a spur-of-the-moment party, informality reigns; keep food simple, serve right from the stove and eat in the kitchen if possible.

If you have a little time to plan, shop and cook, we have a more elaborate menu suggestion: still so easy that any "fool" can cook it. Just don't fiddle around with our soup or get twisted in the rotini.

Fiddley-Dee Fiddlehead Soup, *Page 66*
Rotini With Tomato-Bean Sauce, *Page 133*
Spinach-Grapefruit Salad With Sesame Dressing, *Page 80*
Crusty Rolls
OR
Whole Wheat Bread Sticks, *Page 197*
Wacky Cake, *Page 178*

A classy but informal light luncheon

4 servings

Restaurateurs know that soups and salads are not simply meal accompaniments. Especially at lunch time, they are often the meal. You can cater to this trend when entertaining at home, too. When it is your turn to host the bridge group, or simply for a friendly get-together, a soup and salad or sandwich luncheon provides the sustenance for a good visit.

Cream of Broccoli Soup, *Page 62*
Sesame Crisps, *Page 203*
Chicken Salad Veronique, *Page 124*
Lemon Sponge Pudding, *Page 159*

Mother's Day brunch

4 servings

Rather than fight the restaurant crowds on this busy day, why not treat Mom to a more personal treat — a meal prepared by her offspring; Dad may help too.

Give Mom a book or some special bath oil and banish her from the kitchen. The food needn't be fancy or spectacular; it is best to choose simple recipes that family members can prepare without Mom's guidance. Don't forget to clean up after! Even her favorite flowers on the table won't make amends for a messy kitchen. Here's a wonderful way to start Mom's day:

Fruit Salad With Yogurt Topping, ***Page 163***
Scrambled Eggs With Cream Cheese, ***Page 134***
Home Fries or Hash Browns
Sliced Tomatoes
Toasted English Muffins With Marmalade or Jam

'B' is for barbecues

8 servings

Thanks to gas barbecues, many of us now barbecue year round. However, the spring sunshine brings us outdoors more frequently, and the aromas wafting through the neighborhood whet our appetites and spur us on to more frequently varied barbecued treats.

While barbecues are seldom black tie occasions, the swordfish and minted fruit combo would be appropriate for a special, dress-up event. For a casual barbecue, the short ribs and layered sundae squares will satisfy the heartiest appetites.

Barbecued Swordfish, ***Page 112***
OR
Mining Camp Shortribs, ***Page 96***
Patio Potatoes, ***Page 143***
OR
Baked Potatoes
Foil Wrapped Barbecued Vegetables, ***Page 143***
Greek Salad, ***Page 75***
Minted Oranges and Grapes, ***Page 164***
Layered Sundae Squares, ***Page 170***

Cottage fare

6 servings

For cottagers, the Victoria Day weekend is the traditional cottage-opening weekend. Even when there are no nasty surprises, such as finding that a bureau has become a condominium for mice, there is always lots of work to do.

The fresh air and physical activity are sure to result in hearty appetites. Substantial, but no-fuss meals are appreciated by everyone.

As a change from barbecued meals, take along a prepared, transportable casserole, or one that is easily assembled from convenience foods. Salad ingredients can be cleaned and bagged at home and the dessert should be one that travels and keeps well.

Caesar Salad, *Page 74*
OR
Vegetables With Dips, *Starting Page 39*
Miriam's Chicken Cacciatore, *Page 125*
OR
Camper's Coq Au Vin, *Page 123*
Garlic Bread or Crusty Rolls
Rhubarb Puddle Cake, *Page 175*

Summer is meant for easy living

Summer is the easiest time of the year to entertain; formal dinner parties are in the past or the future.
Get-togethers are more casual and often spontaneous.
Cook and eat al fresco whenever possible so you won't miss any of the glorious, too-short summer.
Fortunately, we don't have to look too far or too hard for the wonderful ingredients of our summer meals — tender vegetables and fresh fruits.

Bridal shower or luncheon

12 - 14 servings

Happy events call for a cheery hostess; that means keeping the food simple and easy to serve. Unless your party is small (for example a luncheon for the bridal party), the food will likely be served buffet style and be eaten from a plate balanced on the knee, so keep it easy to handle and eat, too.

Contemporary Wine Cooler, *Page 53*
Park Avenue Pate, *Page 48*
Maply Appetizers, *Page 35*
Spring Party Sandwich Loaf, *Page 120*
Orange-Blossom Cauliflower, *Page 84*
Tiny Tarts with Lemon Butter Filling, *Page 182*
Jean's Strawberry Devonshire Tart, *Page 182*

Graduation time

8 - 10 servings

A graduation is an occasion worth celebrating. It is both a joyous and a serious event, marking an important stage in the life of a family member or a friend.

A special meal is a good way to say congratulations and best wishes. This menu includes both trendy foods and some favorite, comfort foods.

Celebration Punch, *Page 53*
Vegetables and Dips, *Starting Page 39*
Hummus, *Page 42*
Caesar Salad, *Page 74*
OR
Carrot-Green Pepper Salad, *Page 81*
Beef Balls Bourguignon, *Page 91*
Mandarin Rice, *Page 146*
Rolls
Fruit for a Crowd, *Page 164*
Old-Fashioned Oatmeal Treats, *Page 194*
AND/OR
Chocolate Orange Brownies, *Page 191*

Father's Day

4 servings

This is the day to pamper Dad by serving his favorite foods. With a little help from Mom, the kids should be able to do much of the preparation and cooking for this family-sized menu.

Memory Lane Lemonade, *Page 56*
"Silver Plated" Steak, *Page 99*
OR
Barbecued Spareribs, *Page 108*
Patio Potatoes, *Page 143*
Sesame Herb Bread, *Page 202*
Salad
Rhubarb Cream Pie With Streusel Topping, *Page 184*
OR
Merry-Go-Round Sundaes, *Page 171*

Midsummer night's dream

8 servings

People in northern climates really appreciate the summer solstice — the longest day and shortest night of the year. Our menu includes a traditional Swedish specialty plus the best of Ontario's early summer produce.

Get out your best linens, china and silver and put a bouquet of roses on the table for this very special occasion.

Vichyssoise, *Page 72*
Marinated Salmon, *Page 116*
Dilled Potatoes
Garden-Fresh Leaf Lettuce Salad
With Sweetened Vinegar Dressing, *Page 90*
Steamed Asparagus OR Frenched Green Beans
Strawberries Romanoff, *Page 163*
OR
Jo's Fruit Dip, *Page165*
OR
Gwen's Lime Cheesecake, *Page 160*
garnished with Chocolate Dipped Strawberries, *Page 161*

Summer brunch

6 servings

If your home becomes a bed and breakfast stop for visitors during the summer, make-ahead foods give you a head start. A brunch is a great way to combine a casual meal with a visit.

Sunny Mimosas, ***Page 56***
Sausage and Cheese Strata, ***Page 101***
Yogurt and Blueberry Muffins, ***Page 199***
Fanfare Muffins, ***Page 200***
Sour Cream Coffee Cake, ***Page 204***
Berry-Apricot Brandy Preserves, ***Page 215***
Melon Ball Compote, ***Page 165***
Coffee

Porch or patio luncheon

8 servings

You are the cook; Mother Nature is the decorator, and the birds provide the background music.

The occasion? A meal on the porch, patio or deck shared with good friends. Old-fashioned, roomy porches are wonderful places to sit and enjoy the view while sheltered from the elements.

Since you can't predict the weather, we suggest serving both hot and chilled foods. And be sure to allow generous servings as eating outdoors whets the appetite.

Garden-Fresh Minestrone, ***Page 69***
Composed Peach and Vegetable Salad, ***Page 87***
Pumpernickel Rolls
OR
Whole Wheat Bread Sticks, ***Page 197***
Orange Fruit Dip, ***Page 166***
OR
Fresh Cherry Pie, ***Page 184***

Beyond burgers and steaks

4 - 8 servings

The most modern households are still cooking in the most old-fashioned way — over fire, or more accurately, over hot coals. The coals are heated quickly and easily today with the flick of a switch, but barbecued foods still have that special flavor.

Sangria Blanca, ***Page 57***
Barbecued Lamb Chops, ***Page 108***
OR
Pork Souvlaki, ***Page 107***
Skewered Potatoes and Onions, ***Page 142***
OR
Turkey Burgers, ***Page 130***
With Grilled Onions and Oranges, ***Page 142***
Rye Herb Bread, ***Page 202***
Tossed Salad
Hot Fruit Shortcake, ***Page 156***
OR
Waikiki Pineapple, ***Page 156***

Family picnic

6 - 8 servings

Let the youngsters help with preparing and packing the food for a family outing. You can teach them some valuable food safety lessons and give them some pre-September lunch-making practice.

Include some activity in your picnic plans — a ball game, perhaps, a swim and/or kite-flying. Don't just drive to the picnic location, eat and drive home. Have some fun with your food.

Bloody Mary Soup, ***Page 59***
Chunky Egg Salad With Vegetables, ***Page 134***
Pita Pocket Chicken Salad, ***Page 119***
Ham-Slaw Sandwiches, ***Page 118***
Fresh Fruit
Man-Size Chocolate Chip Cookies, ***Page 187***
OR
Back Packer's Delight, ***Page 190***

Summer time is salad time

6 - 8 servings

Hot humid days can depress our appetites. Something cool and refreshing, but nourishing, is what we need to keep going — at work or play. Salad meals fill the bill beautifully.

Cool Gazpacho, ***Page 61***
Tossed Nicoise Salad, ***Page 77***
Sweet and Sour Beet and Beet Green Salad, ***Page 89***
Crusty Rolls
Warm Blueberry Grunt, ***Page 155***

Bountiful harvest

6 servings

Intensity of flavor and color — that's what we get from really fresh, locally grown vegetables and fruit. Ontario becomes a bountiful garden in summer. Enjoy a drive through the countryside and pick up the ingredients for supper along the way.

Creamy Corn Soup, ***Page 63***
Bread Sticks
OR
Crackers
Italian Meat Pie, ***Page 93***
Ratatouille Provencal, ***Page 146***
OR
Hot Herbed Tomatoes, ***Page 145***
Peach Melba, ***Page 169***

Invigorating autumn

September seems like the start of a new year to many of us. Not only is it the beginning of the school year, but also club programs and other activities that were put "on hold" for the summer months start again. Routine returns to our lives and even meal times become more regular.

Cooler weather stimulates appetites and we relish hearty autumn meals featuring foods from the countryside.

Back-to-school lunches

Children in elementary school are learning the basics of good nutrition. Congratulations to the educators for realizing the importance of nutrition and teaching it as early as kindergarten.

If there are three children in the family who take their lunch to school, by the time the youngest child graduates, someone in the family will have packed at least 8,100 lunches! Is it any wonder that we look for new ideas to make lunches appealing for both the packer and the carrier?

One of the most successful ways to have children eat their lunch is to have them prepare it. Some supervision by a parent can ensure that the child has included a well-liked food from each of the four food groups: grain products, vegetables and fruits, milk products, and meat and alternatives.

Soups are satisfying and can be a valuable nutritive addition to the lunch menu. Sandwiches are usually the foundation of a carried lunch; keep them interesting by adding variety.

Dessert tops off the meal. Very sweet or rich desserts can make one feel sluggish after lunch. Fresh or stewed fruit, cookies, muffins, custard or simple puddings, such as rice pudding, are popular and practical.

Here are some ideas to mix and match:

Quick Corn Chowder, *Page 64*
Chunky Tomato Soup, *Page 64*
Baked Scotch Eggs, *Page 100*
Carrot and Raisin Salad, *Page 80*
Beef Sandwich Filling, *Page 118*
Ila's Bran Muffins, *Page 201*
Oat Bran Muffins, *Page 201*
Eggless Pumpkin Cookies, *Page 185*
Chocolate Chip Zucchini Cupcakes, *Page 172*
Personal Choice Snack Mix, *Page 49*

Country fair fare

6 servings

Enjoy a family day at one of the fall fairs held in most towns and some cities. These fairs, organized by agricultural societies, actually take place all summer and fall. They feature competitions and displays of livestock, all types of produce, baking, crafts and flowers: a wonderful place to see the bounty of our country at its best.

You may not be able to purchase the ingredients of a family dinner at the fair, but you are sure to come home with some wonderful menu ideas and a hearty appetite.

Antipasto, ***Page 209***
Dilled Short Ribs With Carrot Gravy, ***Page 95***
Buttermilk Rolls, ***Page 195***
Salad
Elderberry Pie, ***Page 180***

Indian summer picnic

4 - 6 servings

There is one weekend every autumn when we must get out to enjoy the colors of the countryside. There will be many other sightseers on the roads at the same time, so go prepared with your own picnic lunch or supper. You would also enjoy a picnic after a day at a pick-your-own orchard.

This menu shows you can eat hearty without meat.

Carrot and Orange Soup, ***Page 60***
Tabouli, ***Page 135***
Cheesy Cauliflower and Broccoli Tart, ***Page 132***
OR
Calico Cheese Salad, ***Page 133***
Pita Bread
OR
Crusty Rolls
Spiced Plum Compote, ***Page 157***
Cookies

Giving thanks for the harvest feast

6 - 8 servings

There are apples in three of the following recipes and a variety of squash in two of them (pumpkin is in the squash family). We normally avoid repetition of a food or even foods with similar flavors in a meal, but what better time to enjoy these fruits of the harvest?

Spiced Pineapple Juice Punch, *Page 57*
Curried Apple and Squash Soup, *Page 65*
Roast Turkey With Sausage-Apple Stuffing, *Page 127*
Spiced Prunes, *Page 212*
OR
Cranberry Sauce
Potatoes
Saucy Brussels Sprouts, *Page 138*
Orange Waldorf Salad, *Page 86*
Pumpkin-Pecan Flan With Rich Custard Sauce, *Page 168*

A casual Oktoberfest supper

6 servings

For 10 days every October, our communities of Kitchener and Waterloo open their arms and the doors of the fest-halls to everyone who loves German music and food. Other aspects of German culture are an important part of Oktoberfest, too.

The nationally televised Oktoberfest parade allows those who can't join us to experience the Gemutlichkeit atmosphere. You could extend a Wilkommen by inviting guests to share a hearty but casual German meal with you.

Hot Beer Cheese Dip, Page 40
Succulent Roast Pigtails, 106
OR
Rolled Spareribs, Page 103
Scalloped Potatoes, Page 141
OR
Potato Pancakes, Page 140
Braised Red Cabbage, Page 137
Chocolate-Sauerkraut Fudge Cake a la Mode, Page 173

Little ghosts and goblins party

6 servings

Children look forward all fall to their rendezvous with ghosts and goblins, black cats and witches. The excitement peaks as they dress in all manner of costumes for their annual door-to-door trek through the neighborhood.

There is a trend away from home-made treats and even from "trick or treating" in some areas. A neighborhood party might take the place of going door-to-door, or have a dress rehearsal the weekend before Halloween.

Halloween Makeup, ***Page 51***
Popcorn Cats (Centrepiece or Favors), ***Page 52***
Vegetable Sticks With Dip, ***Starting on Page 39***
Gwen's Cheeseburger Pie, ***Page 92***
Pumpkin Cake, ***Page 176***
Milk

Fall scavenger hunt or road rally

8 servings

Adults like to party and play games too, so we suggest a scavenger hunt, road rally or other activity. Activity is the important word — not just a game of cards or a movie, but something that gets you out and doing. Then you can enjoy a hearty dinner.

Bacon-Onion Stuffed Mushrooms, ***Page 33***
Cider Baked Ham, ***Page 105***
Curried Fruit, ***Page 212***
Herbed Rice Ring, ***Page 148***
Broccoli OR Green Beans
Harvest Spice Cake, ***Page 174***

Sunday afternoon buffet for sports fans

6 servings

The next best thing to being at the ballpark, stadium or arena is watching your favorite team with other like-minded fans. You could try to duplicate the game atmosphere by serving only hotdogs and beer, but fans will appreciate your efforts to make a meal worth cheering about.

Curried Party Nibblers, ***Page 50***
Chunky Chili, ***Page 98***
Neighbor's 24 Hour Salad, ***Page 76***
Whole Wheat Bread Sticks, ***Page 197***
Pat's Dutch Apple Pie, ***Page 183***

Festive cocktail party

12 - 15 servings

When the bright colors of early autumn give way to the grey skies of November, we begin to think cheery thoughts of holiday entertaining.

Entertaining and the holiday season just naturally go together. It is a time to renew old friendships and get to know new friends and neighbors better.

Holiday Grape Punch, ***Page 54***
AND/OR
White Wine
Bouchees With Chicken or Beef Filling, ***Page 38***
Corned Beef and Cheese Ball, ***Page 44***
Hot Crab Dip, ***Page 40***
Rum Balls, ***Page 188***
Anise Crescents, ***Page 185***
Creme de Menthe Bars, ***Page 192***
Specialty Coffee or Tea

Winter: We love it or leave it

Canadians either love winter and winter sports, or head south to avoid it. If you aren't a winter sports enthusiast and can't go away, decorate your home and brighten the darkest, coldest months of the year with good food and good cheer.

The "holiday" season extends from St. Nicholas's Day in early December, through January and into February, with the Chinese New Year and Valentine's Day. It ends with Mardi Gras — that great celebration prior to the self-denial and sacrifices of Lent.

Christmas Eve supper/buffet

6 servings

On Christmas Eve, serve a meal that's easy on the cook.

Cranberry Punch, ***Page 54***
Tourtiere, ***Page 104***
OR
Seafood Casserole, ***Page 117***
Sweet and Sour Tossed Salad, ***Page 79***
Dinner Rolls
Mincemeat Flambe, ***Page 153***

Yule brunch

6 servings

The big day has arrived -- usually too quickly for adult family members and too slowly for the children.

Every family has their own gift-opening and meal-time traditions, and these evolve as family ages and size changes. Two hearty meals on Christmas day, brunch and a late afternoon feast, works best for us.

Tropical Ambrosia, ***Page 45***
Lobster or Ham Crepes, ***Page 114***
OR
Crab and Mushroom Quiche, ***Page 113***
Audrey's Salad, ***Page 73***
Apple Brown Betty With Honey, ***Page 149***
OR
Squares

Christmas wish list

The following is our Christmas wish for every host and hostess:

May the turkey be done to perfection;
may the salads be crisp and tasty;
may everyone eat and drink to satisfaction,
and no more;
may the fellowship be seasoned with love;
and may someone else do the dishes.

Christmas feast

8 - 10 servings

Microwave ovens have given us some new variations to our traditional holiday menu.

Roast Turkey With Wild Rice Stuffing, ***Page 128***
OR
Microwave Bread Stuffing, ***Page 128***
Cranberry Chutney, ***Page 211***
Turnip and Apple Casserole, ***Page 145***
OR
Sweet Potatoes a l'Orange, ***Page 144***
French Peas a la Microwave, ***Page 138***
Crunchy Mandarin Salad, ***Page 85***
OR
Moulded Carrot and Raisin Salad, ***Page 82***
Hot Rolls
Carrot Pudding With Brown Sugar Sauce, ***Page 152***

Boxing Day leftovers

6 servings

This is a day to relax and enjoy leftovers. Meals can be as simple as soup and a sandwich, or use leftover turkey in a variety of quick main dishes.

French Onion Soup, ***Page 67***
Hot Swiss Turkey Sandwich Filling, ***Page 122***
California Turkey Melts, ***Page 121***
Monte Cristo Sandwiches, ***Page 122***
Turkey Curry, ***Page 130***
Good-Bye Turkey, ***Page 129***
Christmas Cake, Cookies or Squares

Holiday open house

15-18 servings

An open house is a great way to visit with a number of friends and neighbors at one time. During this busy season, people appreciate being able to drop in for a brief visit before or after another function.

Some will come and stay, however, so don't invite more people than you can comfortably accommodate, on the assumption that there will be a continuous turnover of guests.

Creamy Yule Nog, ***Page 55***
AND
Non-Alcoholic Drinks
Spanakopittas, ***Page 37***
Keftethes (Greek Meat Balls), ***Page 34***
Potted Crabmeat, ***Page 47***
Hot and Zesty Artichoke Dip, ***Page 39***
Smoked Salmon Pate, ***Page 48***
Edam Bowl, ***Page 43***
Christmas Cookies
Specialty Coffee

New Year's resolutions

4 - 6 servings

How many times have you made the same old New Year's resolution — to go on a diet and to spend less money? Healthy eating is a desirable goal for all year, not just the first week of January.

Meals without meat help to control fat intake and may be less expensive.

Vegetables With Creamy But Low-Fat Dips, ***Page 41***
Soup Paysanne, ***Page 71***
Vegetarian Chili, ***Page 136***
Hearty Multi-Grain Bread, ***Page 196***
Deli Cole-Slaw, ***Page 90***
Hot Fudge Pudding, ***Page 158***

Apres ski (skate or toboggan) buffet

4 - 6 servings

Both of the main dish suggestions for this menu can be made in advance, frozen and reheated at your ski chalet or winterized cottage for an easy, satisfying meal.

Mulled Cider, ***Page 58***
OR
Spiced Tea
Cheese Tray With Salami and Apple Wedges
Easy Curried Beef, ***Page 97***
OR
Osso Bucco, ***Page 111***
Rice or Noodles
Salad With Lemony Sour Cream Dressing, ***Page 78***
Crusty French Bread
Chocolate Fondue, ***Page 158***

Winter fireside 'picnic'

2 - 4 servings

A casual, light meal in front of the fire can be the perfect finale to a dreary winter day.

Mulled Cider, ***Page 58***
OR
Spiced Tea
Cheese Fondue, ***Page 131***
Deep Dish Apple Crisp, ***Page 151***
OR
Microwave Apple Crisp, ***Page 151***

Candlelight dinner for two

Valentine's Day is one of the busiest days of the year for restaurateurs. If you would prefer a quiet, romantic evening for just the two of you, treat your Valentine to a meal you have prepared yourself.

Grapefruit Avocado Appetizer, ***Page 45***
Beef Medallions With Wine Sauce, ***Page 94***
Duchesse Potatoes, ***Page 140***
Vegetable Medley
OR
Salad
Baked Apples Flambe, ***Page 150***

Family pancake supper

"Mardi Gras" is how the French-speaking settlers in Louisiana translated "Fat Tuesday," the last day before Lent, when we supposedly practise some self-denial.

Pancakes have been the traditional fare for Fat or Shrove Tuesday for centuries.

Both pancakes and their toppings can be a nutritional challenge. We have included pancake recipes using whole wheat or graham flour and wheat germ for added fibre and nutrients, and fruit toppings as well as syrups. Balance the day's food intake by giving special consideration to what you eat at the other meals on Shrove Tuesday.

Although we call this a supper, pancakes are wonderful at any meal, and the fruit-filled puffy pancake would even be an impressive company dessert.

Choose any of the following recipes that appeal to you and your family. Feel free to mix and match any of the pancakes with a topping given for another.

Guilt-Free Pancakes With Fruit and Yogurt Topping, ***Page 207***
Bill's Pancakes, ***Page 206***
Wheat Germ and Raisin Pancakes With Hot Lemon Syrup, ***Page 208***
Cottage Cheese Pancakes, ***Page 206***
Sour Cream Pancakes, ***Page 205***
Fruit-Filled Puffy Pancake, ***Page 154***

TOPPINGS

Mandarin Sauce, ***Page 214***
Poached Apples and Pears With Cinnamon, ***Page 149***
Easy Maple Flavored Syrup, ***Page 214***
Mock Maple Syrup, ***Page 214***

Cook's Notes

APPETIZERS & SNACKS

Bacon-Onion Stuffed Mushrooms

Mushrooms can be stuffed, covered and refrigerated early in the day and cooked when needed.

Makes 18 - 24

5 - 6 slices side bacon
18 - 24 mushrooms
1/2 cup finely chopped green onion
125 g cream cheese, at room temperature
2 tbsp. fine, dry bread crumbs

Place bacon on a microwavable rack; cover with wax paper to prevent spattering. Cook on High power until crisp (four to six minutes). Rotate pan one-quarter turn during cooking if necessary. Remove bacon and crumble when cool enough to handle. Caution: Paper towels made of recycled paper may catch fire.

Meanwhile, brush or rinse mushrooms; remove and chop stems. Place chopped stems and green onions in a glass two-cup measure; cook on High for two minutes. Stir in cream cheese until well blended; add bread crumbs and crumbled bacon and stir to mix well.

Stuff mushroom caps with cheese mixture and cook on High for four minutes, turning dish during cooking if necessary.

If preferred, cook mushrooms in two batches, about three minutes each, so all mushrooms will be hot when served.

Keftethes (Greek Meat Balls)

Makes 3 dozen

3 tbsp. fine, dry bread crumbs
1/4 cup milk
1 1/2 tbsp. olive oil
2 green onions, finely chopped
1/4 cup finely chopped parsley
1 clove garlic, minced
.5 kg (1 lb.) lean ground beef
1 egg yolk
1 tsp. salt
Freshly ground black pepper
1 tbsp. butter
1 1/2 tbsp. red wine vinegar
1/4 tsp. crumbled dried oregano

Combine bread crumbs and milk and set aside.

Heat oil in a large, heavy skillet and saute onions, parsley and garlic until soft. Combine beef, egg yolk, softened crumbs, salt, pepper and sauteed vegetables. Form meat mixture into one-inch balls.

Add butter to skillet, and more oil if necessary; saute meat balls, turning to brown evenly. Reduce heat and cook gently, stirring frequently until meat is cooked (12 to 15 minutes). Remove meatballs with a slotted spoon and place in serving dish.

Pour vinegar into skillet and heat a few minutes, scraping up the browned drippings.

Sprinkle oregano over meat, then pour the pan drippings over all. Serve warm.

Maply Appetizers

Makes 2 - 3 dozen

1 can (14 oz./398 ml) pineapple chunks
500 g brown and serve sausages*
4 tsp. cornstarch
1/2 tsp. salt
1/2 cup maple syrup
1/3 cup water
1/3 cup white vinegar
1 large green pepper, cut in chunks
1/2 cup maraschino cherries, drained

* Or substitute 25 to 30 small meatballs, cooked, OR cocktail wieners OR thickly sliced smoked sausages.

Drain pineapple, reserving juice. Cut sausages in thirds; brown in skillet.

Blend cornstarch, salt, pineapple juice, maple syrup, water and vinegar. Heat to boiling, stirring constantly. Add pineapple chunks, sausage pieces, green pepper and cherries; cook gently five minutes. Keep warm in chafing dish. Spear with cocktail picks.

Mushroom Tarts

Makes 12 regular or 24 tiny tarts

Pastry for a two-crust pie or frozen tart shells (12 regular or 24 mini)
3 tbsp. butter or margarine
1 onion, finely chopped
2 tbsp. flour
1 can (10 oz./284 mL) sliced mushrooms
2 tbsp. lemon juice or dry sherry
Water
2 tsp. snipped fresh parsley
1/4 tsp. thyme
1/4 tsp. salt (optional)
Dash pepper
1/4 cup sour cream
5 - 6 stuffed olives, sliced

Roll out pastry and cut into rounds to fit tart pans. Or thaw frozen tart shells.

Heat butter and saute onion until soft and just beginning to brown. Sprinkle with flour; cook and stir until flour is well blended.

Drain mushrooms, reserving liquid. Add lemon juice or sherry to mushroom liquid, plus enough water to make one cup liquid. Add liquid, parsley, thyme, salt and pepper to onion mixture. Cook, stirring frequently, until sauce is thickened. Add mushrooms and cook gently about three minutes. Remove from heat; stir in sour cream.

Spoon filling into tart shells. Bake at 400 degrees F for 10 to 12 minutes. Garnish with olive slices and serve hot.

Note: Tarts may be frozen before baking. Bake without thawing for 25 minutes at 400 degrees F.

Spanakopittas

Once made, these delicious Greek appetizers can be frozen, then baked when needed.

Makes about 50

3 cups finely chopped fresh spinach
3/4 cup chopped fresh dill weed
3/4 cup chopped green onions
2 tbsp. salt
1 medium onion, finely chopped
1/4 cup olive oil
1 cup crumbled feta cheese
1/2 cup grated Parmesan cheese
1 egg, slightly beaten
1 tbsp. crumbled dried mint
2 packages (1 lb./454 g each) filo, thawed
Unsalted butter, melted

Wash and dry spinach ahead of time, so the filling won't be too watery. Combine spinach, dill and green onions in large mixing bowl; sprinkle with salt. Knead the vegetables, then let sit five to 10 minutes to draw out liquid. Meanwhile, saute onion in oil, about five minutes.

Drain vegetable mixture and press out as much liquid as possible. Stir spinach mixture, cheeses, egg and mint into cooked onion. Set filling aside.

The best way to defrost the filo is to leave the package overnight in the refrigerator; it thaws slowly and won't crack easily. Or remove it from its carton but not out of the plastic bag and leave at room temperature at least two hours.

Lay filo out flat; cut in half, crosswise. Rewrap half of the sheets, using only 15 or so at a time. While working with the filo, always keep it covered with a slightly dampened cloth. (Once pastry has dried, it cannot be folded.) Take one sheet of filo; lay it on a clean, dry surface, and fold into thirds, lengthwise. Brush with melted butter.

Place a scant tablespoon of filling on top left hand corner; pick up corner and bring it over to the right to meet the bottom edge and form a triangle (if filling oozes out, let it). Continue to fold towards right end of strip, always forming a triangle. Before you make the final fold, brush with melted butter.

Place completed triangles on oiled cookie sheets, seam side down. Brush tops with melted butter, then bake at 350 degrees F for 25 to 30 minutes or until puffy and lightly browned.

Bouchees (Choux Paste)

Bouchees or cream puffs look elaborate, but only the cook knows how quickly and easily they can be prepared.

Puff or choux paste is simply a very thick white sauce with extra butter and eggs beaten in. The dough is thick enough to hold its shape when dropped onto a baking sheet. The eggs make the puffs swell as they cook and the high cooking temperature sets the crust before all the air inside the puff can escape. This creates a handy cavity.

Tiny puffs or bouchees with a savory filling are used as appetizers. If you add a small amount of sugar to the basic paste and bake large puffs, you can fill them with cream or custard, glaze them with a chocolate sauce and serve as dessert.

Makes 60 bouchees or 14 large puffs

1 cup all purpose flour
1 cup water
1/4 tsp. salt
1/2 cup butter
4 eggs, at room temperature

Measure flour and set aside. Put water, salt and butter in saucepan and heat until butter is melted. Heat to a full rolling boil; add flour all at once. Remove from heat. Stir until mixture becomes a very thick paste that clings together and pulls away from the sides of the pan.

Add eggs, one at a time, beating after each addition. Beat until paste is smooth and glossy.

Drop one-half to one teaspoon dough per bouchee (one-quarter cup per large puff) onto ungreased cookie sheets. Bake in a preheated 400 degree F oven 20 to 25 minutes (35 to 40 minutes for larger size). When baked, they should feel very light but firm to the touch, and be light golden brown in color. Turn off oven.

It is advisable to make a small slit in the side of each puff to allow steam to escape. Return to oven for five to 10 minutes to allow centres to dry.

CHICKEN OR BEEF FILLING

1 cup diced cooked chicken or beef
1/4 cup finely diced celery
2 tbsp. finely chopped green pepper

1 - 2 tbsp. finely chopped pimento
1/4 tsp. Worcestershire sauce
1/4 tsp. lemon juice
1 tsp. grated onion
1/4 tsp. salt
1/8 tsp. pepper
1/3 cup mayonnaise

Combine all of the above ingredients. Chill. Use to fill bouchees.

Hot, Zesty Artichoke Dip

1 can (14 oz./398 ml) artichoke hearts
1 cup grated Parmesan cheese
1 cup mayonnaise
Dash each of garlic powder, Worcestershire sauce and Tabasco
Parsley
Paprika

Drain artichokes thoroughly and mash. Mix together cheese, mayonnaise, garlic powder, Worcestershire and Tabasco sauces; fold in artichokes.

Spoon mixture into a one-litre casserole and bake until hot and bubbly at 325 degrees F (about 20 minutes).

Garnish dip with a small amount of freshly snipped parsley and sprinkle lightly with paprika. Serve warm with crackers.

Hot Beer-Cheese Dip

This peppy dip is easy but impressive. It combines popular flavors and goes well with a variety of autumn fruits, vegetables and crackers.

Makes $1\frac{3}{4}$ cups

250 g cream cheese
1 cup grated cheddar cheese
$\frac{1}{3}$ cup beer
1 tsp. dried or 1 tbsp. fresh chives
$\frac{1}{2}$ tsp. dry mustard
1 tsp. horseradish
Dash cayenne pepper

Melt cheeses in a one-litre microwavable casserole on 50% power (Medium or Medium Low) for four to $4\frac{1}{2}$ minutes, stirring after two minutes. Stir in beer, chives, dry mustard and horseradish. Cover with lid or vented plastic wrap. Cook on 50% power for six to seven minutes or until bubbly, stirring twice during cooking. Pour into a serving dish that can be placed on a hot tray or returned to the microwave oven if necessary; sprinkle with cayenne.

Serve warm with crackers, raw vegetables or apple or pear wedges.

Hot Crab Dip

Makes $2\frac{1}{2}$ cups

250 g cream cheese, softened
1 can (4.25 oz./120 g) crab meat, drained
$\frac{1}{4}$ cup chopped onion
1 tbsp. lemon juice
1 tbsp. Worcestershire sauce
$\frac{1}{2}$ tsp. horseradish, drained
2 - 4 tbsp. sliced almonds

Combine cream cheese, crab meat, onion, lemon juice, Worcestershire sauce and horseradish. Turn into a small, buttered casserole or two onion soup bowls; sprinkle with sliced almonds. Bake at 350 degrees F for 15 minutes, or until bubbly. Serve with crackers or vegetables.

> **Note:** Onion soup bowls make attractive serving dishes. Keep one warm while the other is served.

Creamy But Low-Fat Dips

Creamy dips have become a North American entertaining staple, and we recognize and appreciate the nutritional value of the veggies that accompany them. In keeping with the latest nutrition recommendations to reduce our fat intake, we adapt our old familiar dips and spreads to use low-fat products wherever possible.

CURRY VEGETABLE DIP

Makes about 2 cups

1 1/2 cups light salad dressing
3 tbsp. light sour cream
1/2 tsp. salt
Dash pepper
1 - 2 tsp. curry powder (to taste)
1/2 tsp. dry mustard
1 - 2 dashes of Worcestershire or Tabasco sauce
1 tbsp. grated onion

Combine all ingredients in a bowl and blend thoroughly. Chill for several hours before serving. Keeps for one week.

SLENDER-BLENDER VEGETABLE DIP

Makes about 1 1/4 cups

1 cup low-fat cottage cheese
2 tbsp. yogurt or mayonnaise
2 green onions, finely chopped
1 clove garlic, minced
1 tbsp. pickle relish
2 tsp. Worcestershire sauce
1 tsp. paprika
1 tsp. prepared mustard

Combine all ingredients in a blender or food processor and blend thoroughly. Chill. Place dip in a bowl in the centre of a tray or large plate. Surround dip with a selection of carrot, rutabaga and celery sticks, green pepper, cucumber and zucchini slices, cherry tomatoes or tomato wedges, radishes, whole mushrooms, green onions, cauliflower and broccoli flowerettes.

Hummus

Makes about 3 cups

1 cup dried chick peas
OR 1 can (19 oz./540 ml) chick peas, drained
$^{1}/_{2}$ tsp. salt
2 - 3 large cloves garlic, peeled
$^{1}/_{4}$ cup snipped fresh parsley
Juice of $1^{1}/_{2}$ medium lemons (about $^{1}/_{3}$ cup)
$^{1}/_{2}$ tsp. tamari or soy sauce
$^{1}/_{4}$ tsp. ground cumin
$^{1}/_{4}$ tsp. black or lemon pepper
Dash of cayenne
$^{1}/_{2}$ cup tahini*
3 green onions, coarsely chopped
$^{1}/_{2}$ - $^{2}/_{3}$ cup low-fat plain yogurt

* This sesame seed paste is available in natural food stores.

Place chick peas in medium saucepan; cover with cold water and soak $1^{1}/_{2}$ hours. Heat to boiling, add more water if needed, cover pan and simmer $1^{1}/_{2}$ hours, or until chick peas are soft. Drain well.

Puree cooked chick peas in food processor; with motor running, add salt, garlic, parsley, lemon juice, tamari, cumin, pepper and cayenne. Scrape down sides of bowl and add tahini, green onions and yogurt. Process until well blended.

Put hummus in a bowl, cover and chill two to three hours, or up to four days. Garnish with a twist of orange rind and serve with pieces of pita bread and raw vegetables.

Note: If a food processor or blender is not available, mash chick peas until very smooth and beat in all remaining ingredients.

Edam Bowl

The bright red paraffin wax coating of Edam cheese makes it a natural for the festive season. It you are artistic, decorate the outside of the cheese to look like a Santa face, for an edible table decoration.

15 or more servings

850 g ball of Edam cheese
1/2 cup mayonnaise or salad dressing
1/2 cup chutney
1/2 tsp. curry powder

Do not remove the wax coating from the cheese, but cut a slice off the top. Scoop out most of the cheese, leaving a shell about one-half inch thick. An apple corer is a good tool to get this process started.

In a food processor, combine the pieces of cheese with mayonnaise, chutney and curry powder.

Process until finely chopped and well mixed. (If you don't have a food processor, shred the cheese and then mix in remaining ingredients.)

Spoon mixture back into shell (there will be more filling than the cheese will hold; refrigerate extra and refill cheese as needed). Cover cheese with plastic wrap and refrigerate until 30 minutes before the party.

Place on a tray with a small knife and a variety of crackers or crisp breads, apple slices and/or celery sticks.

Corned Beef and Cheese Ball

The flavor of this meaty cheeseball improves on standing, so make it a day or two before your party.

2 1/2 - 3 inch diameter ball

125 g cream cheese, softened
1 cup grated cheddar cheese
1 can (12 oz./340 g) corned beef, shredded
1 tsp. horseradish
1 tsp. prepared mustard
1/4 tsp. Worcestershire sauce
1/4 tsp. grated lemon rind
2 tbsp. lemon juice
1/3 cup sweet pickle relish, drained
1/2 cup snipped fresh parsley

In a mixer bowl or food processor, blend together thoroughly: cheeses, corned beef, horseradish, mustard, Worcestershire sauce, lemon rind and juice and pickle relish.

Cover or wrap and refrigerate at least 30 minutes or until firm enough to shape.

Shape into a ball or log and roll in parsley until completely coated. Wrap or cover loosely, so you don't disturb the parsley.

Refrigerate again, until just before ready to serve with assorted crackers.

Tropical Ambrosia

Ambrosial ambrosia can be served as an appetizer or dessert at brunch or dinner.

6 servings

$1\frac{1}{2}$ grapefruits, sectioned
$\frac{1}{4}$ cup shredded coconut, divided
2 oranges, sectioned or sliced
1 banana, sliced
1 kiwi fruit, peeled and sliced
Amaretto liqueur (optional)

Place half the grapefruit sections in a serving bowl. Sprinkle with one tablespoon coconut. Add orange sections and banana slices; sprinkle with two tablespoons coconut. Add remaining grapefruit sections and coconut. Top with half circles of kiwi fruit. Drizzle with Amaretto if desired. Cover and chill.

Grapefruit-Avocado Appetizer

2 servings

2 tbsp. honey
$\frac{1}{2}$ tsp. poppy seeds
1 grapefruit
$\frac{1}{2}$ avocado

Heat honey over hot water or by microwave; add poppy seeds.

Halve grapefruit and remove each segment; place in bowl. Squeeze juice from grapefuit and add to honey mixture.

Cut avocado in half; remove stone. Peel one half of avocado. (Running a grapefruit knife just under the skin is the easiest method we've found.) Slice peeled avocado lengthwise into strips and cut crosswise into bite-size chunks; add to grapefruit. Pour liquid over fruit; stir gently, cover and refrigerate until serving time.

> **Note:** Brush cut surface of other half of avocado with lemon juice, cover with plastic wrap and refrigerate.

Perfect partners

Together, the flavors and colors of this two-part appetizer are very complementary, but either could be used alone or matched with other appetizers. Both parts can be made a day or two before serving.

SALSA ASPIC RING

About 1 1/2 cups

1 envelope unflavored gelatine
1/4 cup water
1 jar (375 mL) salsa sauce*
2 tsp. horseradish
1/4 tsp. Worcestershire sauce

*With the added horseradish and Worcestershire sauce, mild salsa is just right for our taste buds.

Dissolve the gelatine in hot water, or soften it in cold water, according to package directions. Heat salsa to boiling in a four-cup glass measure or small saucepan. Remove from microwave (or from heat) and stir in horseradish, Worcestershire sauce and dissolved or softened gelatine

Rinse a small ring mould (about three-cup capacity) with cold water or brush very lightly with vegetable oil. Pour in salsa mixture and chill until set. Cover with plastic or foil wrap and return to refrigerator until ready to serve.

Run a knife around outer and inner edges of mould; dip mould into hot water for 30 to 60 seconds and unmould onto serving plate. Fill centre with crab meat dip, dip of your choice, vegetables, olives or pickles. Serve with crackers.

CRAB MEAT DIP

About 1 3/4 cups

1 can (4.25 oz./120 g) crab meat, drained
2 tbsp. lemon juice
250 g cream cheese, at room temperature
1/4 cup mayonnaise
1 tbsp. minced onion
1 green onion, sliced
1 tsp. Worcestershire sauce

Pick any pieces of shell or cartilage out of crab meat. Place in a small bowl and stir in lemon juice; let marinate at room temperature for 30 minutes. Cream the cheese; beat in mayonnaise. Stir in onion, green onion and Worcestershire sauce. Thoroughly blend in crab meat (do not drain off lemon juice). Cover and chill.

Use dip to fill centre of salsa ring (put it in a small bowl if you have one that fits the opening). Serve with crackers.

Potted Crabmeat

Makes about 3 cups

2 cans (4.25 oz./120 g each) crabmeat
500 g cream cheese, at room temperature
1/4 cup mayonnaise
1/4 tsp. curry powder
1 1/2 tbsp. finely minced onion
2 tsp. lemon juice
1/2 tsp. Worcestershire sauce

Drain crabmeat and remove any pieces of shell or cartilage. Place crab meat, cheese, mayonnaise, curry powder, onion, lemon juice and Worcestershire sauce in food processor (or deep mixing bowl) and mix well.

Press crabmeat mixture into a lightly oiled small mould.

If prepared a day or two in advance, store in mould, covered tightly with plastic wrap, in refrigerator. For serving within a few hours, unmould onto serving dish, cover loosely and chill until needed.

Garnish potted crabmeat with parsley and/or pimento and serve with crackers and/or celery.

Smoked Salmon Pate

Makes about 2 cups

6 oz. (150 - 175 g) salmon fillet
Salt
Freshly ground black pepper
3 tbsp. dry white wine
2 tbsp. cream cheese
6 oz. (150 - 175 g) smoked salmon, cut into small pieces
1 tbsp. lemon juice
1/2 tsp. dry mustard

Place salmon fillet in the middle of a piece of foil large enough to enclose it. Season with salt, pepper and wine. Enclose fillet in foil and seal tightly. Place a steamer basket in a pot of water (water should come just below the level of the basket). When water boils, add salmon and steam seven to eight minutes, or until fish flakes. Cool, drain and remove skin.

Place cooked salmon in food processor. Add cheese, smoked salmon, lemon juice and mustard. Process just until combined. Spoon into serving bowl, cover and chill. Serve with crackers.

Park Avenue Pate

Makes two 6-oz. ramekins

.5 kg (1 lb.) chicken livers
1 medium onion, sliced
1/4 cup chopped onion OR green onion
1 tsp. dry mustard
2 tbsp. dry sherry or brandy
1/2 cup butter, softened
Pinch of mace
Salt and pepper to taste
1/4 - 1/2 cup chopped ham
2 - 4 tbsp. table cream (18% M.F.)

Simmer chicken livers and sliced onion in water to cover, about 20 minutes. Drain livers; discard onion and liquid. Chop livers very fine in food processor. Add chopped onion, mustard, sherry, butter, mace, salt, pepper and ham and process until well blended. Add cream gradually until pate is spreadable; pate will stiffen on refrigeration. If mixture is too dry, it will crumble when cut or spread. Spoon pate into ramekins, cover and refrigerate until serving time. Use within one week.

To serve: Spread pate on toast triangles, bread or crackers. Pate may also be sliced and served (two to three slices/person) as an appetizer for a sit-down dinner.

Personal Choice Snack Mix

You can put a personal imprint on the popular snack mix called Nuts and Bolts. You can control the amount of sodium and flavoring and cater to your own family's taste preferences in the ingredients used.

You can add or substitute puffed rice, wheat or corn cereal for the cereals listed, but keep the proportions the same.

Makes 10 - 12 cups

1/2 cup margarine or butter
1 - 2 tsp. Worcestershire sauce
Dash garlic powder
Dash onion powder
1/2 tsp. seasoned salt or barbecue spice
4 cups Cheerios*
2 cups Shreddies or Crispix*****
4 cups pretzel sticks (break into 1 1/2-inch pieces if necessary)
1 - 3 cups unsalted peanuts or mixed nuts

*Registered trademark used with permission of General Mills Canada Inc.

** Registered trademark of Nabisco Brands Ltd.

*** Registered trademark of Kellogg Canada Inc.

Put margarine in a large roasting pan and place in the oven while preheating oven to 250 degrees F. Stir in Worcestershire sauce, garlic and onion powders and salt.

Add cereals, pretzels and nuts, and toss to coat with seasoned margarine. Cover pan and bake at 250 degrees F for one hour, stirring once.

Uncover and bake 30 minutes longer, stirring occasionally.

Cool completely, then store mix in air-tight containers.

Curried Party Nibblers

Smaller quantities of snack mix can be prepared in a microwave oven. This one has a peppy flavor.

About 6 cups

1/3 cup margarine
1 tsp. curry powder
1 tsp. garlic powder
1/2 tsp. onion powder
1/2 tsp. ginger
1/2 tsp. celery seed
1/2 tsp. soy sauce
1 1/2 tbsp. Worcestershire sauce
1 cup peanuts
1 cup chow mein noodles
2 cups Shreddies*
2 cups Cheerios breakfast cereal**

*Registered trademark of Nabisco Brands Ltd.

**Registered trademark used with permission of General Mills Canada Inc.

In a three-litre microwavable bowl, melt margarine on High power for one minute. Add spices, soy sauce and Worcestershire sauce. Stir to blend well.

Add peanuts, chow mein noodles, Shreddies and Cheerios and stir until well coated with seasoned margarine. Heat on High for five to six minutes, stirring after three minutes, then every minute.

Cool completely and store in an air-tight container.

Halloween Makeup

Many years ago the Waterloo Public Library sent out a flyer with this recipe on it. Craft books with other makeup and costume ideas may be available at your library.

Enough for 1 - 2 faces

2 tsp. shortening, room temperature
5 tsp. cornstarch
1 tsp. flour
Few drops vegetable oil
Food coloring

Using a small bowl and a fork, mix shortening, cornstarch and flour until smooth. For a creamy consistency, blend in 3 to 4 drops of oil. Now stir in food coloring, adding only one to two drops at a time until desired shade is realized. Cover the face with makeup before adding dramatic effects.

For brown accent lines: Combine 1 tsp. shortening and $2^1/_2$ tsp. cocoa. Blend in 2 - 3 drops oil. Apply with a makeup brush.

For witch's or monster's warts: Combine 1 tsp. peanut butter with about 1 tsp. desiccated coconut. Stick on face in small blobs. Use a pale green or white makeup base on face before adding warts.

For a mummy: Wrap face with gauze, leaving lots of space around eyes, nose and mouth. Then apply desired shade of makeup base. Pat some oatmeal on the cheeks. Using a dark red lipstick, make a gash on one side of face. Dust with talcum powder.

Whatever makeup you use, be sure your child can see clearly.

Popcorn Balls

$^{1}/_{2}$ cup popping corn, popped
$^{1}/_{2}$ cup sugar
$^{1}/_{2}$ tsp. salt
$^{1}/_{2}$ cup corn syrup

Combine sugar, salt and corn syrup in a large saucepan (three to four litres). Mix thoroughly and heat until sugar is dissolved. Add popcorn; cook and stir over medium heat until corn is completely coated. Remove from heat.

With oiled hands shape into popcorn balls of desired size.

OR use the mixture to make the following . . . .

Popcorn Cat

1 large popcorn ball (see above recipe)
1 small popcorn ball
6 black pipe cleaners
2 round green ju jubes or gum drops
1 round black ju jube or gum drop
Toothpicks

Place smaller ball on top of larger one, fastening them together with toothpicks.

For whiskers: Use two pipe cleaners, cut in three equal lengths (three on each side). Bend tips at one end and insert into popcorn. Add green ju jubes for eyes and a black one for the nose in suitable positions using half a toothpick for each.

Bend one pipe cleaner for ears (adjust to proper length).

For tail: Place three remaining pipe cleaners side by side; twist gently together and bend in half. Insert tail and bend upwards above side or bottom of large ball.

BEVERAGES

Celebration Punch

16 servings

1 can (48 oz./1.36 L) pineapple juice, chilled
1 can (48 oz./1.36 L) orange-grapefruit juice, chilled
2 bottles (750 mL each) lemon-lime soda, chilled
500 g lime sherbet

Mix juices and lemon-lime soda in a large punch bowl.

Just before serving, add sherbet, using an ice-cream scoop if possible.

Serve immediately. For a very pretty effect, serve this non-alcoholic punch in tall wine glasses.

Contemporary Wine Cooler

You can make your own wine cooler for pleasant sipping before or with meals.

15 - 18 servings

1 1/3 cups sugar
3 cups water
8 whole cloves
3 - 4 cinnamon sticks, broken
4 slices fresh ginger root
3 lemons, thinly sliced
2 bottles (750 mL or 1 L each) sauternes*
Ice cubes

*Or substitute a white table wine with a sweetness rating of two.

Combine sugar, water, cloves, cinnamon, ginger root and two lemons in a saucepan or large microwavable bowl. Heat just to boiling, then simmer for 10 to 15 minutes, stirring occasionally to dissolve sugar. Strain syrup and cool.

Mix cooled syrup with wine; add remaining sliced lemon and ice.

Cranberry Punch

Makes about 24 4-oz. servings

1 L cranberry cocktail
750 mL white grape juice
3/4 cup grapefruit juice concentrate, thawed not diluted
1 - 2 cups white rum, optional
750 mL gingerale
1 orange, thinly sliced
1 lemon, thinly sliced
1 lime, thinly sliced (optional)

Chill all juices, rum and gingerale.

Place ice cubes in punch bowl. Add fruit juices and rum, if used; stir. Add gingerale and float fruit slices on top.

Holiday Grape Punch

12 - 16 servings

2 cups water
1/2 cup sugar
1 1/2 tsp. anise seeds
2 tsp. whole cloves
12 cups purple grape juice (bottled or reconstituted frozen concentrate)
1/4 cup lemon juice
2 bottles (750 mL each) club soda
1 - 1 1/2 cups white rum (optional)
Ice cubes

In saucepan, combine water, sugar, anise seeds and cloves. Heat to boiling; reduce heat and simmer five minutes. Cool.

Strain syrup into punch bowl. Add grape and lemon juices.

Just before serving, stir in club soda, rum if used, and add ice cubes.

Creamy Yule Nog

In this, or any recipe including raw eggs, be sure to use eggs with clean, uncracked shells. Utensils for mixing must be clean and all perishable ingredients at refrigerator temperature. Be sure to serve eggnog well chilled!

Makes about 8 cups

250 mL whipping cream
4 eggs, separated
1 cup sugar
1/2 cup rye whisky (optional)
1 oz. rum (optional)
250 mL table cream (18% M.F.)
3/4 cup milk
Ground nutmeg

Beat whipping cream until thick (not stiff); set aside.

In large mixer bowl, beat egg yolks and sugar thoroughly. Add whisky and blend. Spoon whipped cream into egg mixture and beat until smooth; add rum, table cream and milk and mix well.

Whip egg whites until stiff but not dry. Fold into egg yolk/cream mixture. Whisk lightly to eliminate any "clumps" of egg white and to ensure the nog is smooth.

Cover and chill thoroughly. Whisk again just before serving and sprinkle with nutmeg.

Memory Lane Lemonade

Ever since some imaginative person looked at an orange and a lemon and decided it would be fun to squeeze them, citrus drinks have been one of the world's favorite refreshments.

Makes 5 cups

6 lemons
3 oranges
2 limes
3 cups boiling water
3/4 cup sugar (or to taste)

Squeeze 5 1/2 of the lemons, 2 1/2 oranges and 1 1/2 limes, reserving all juices and lemon "shells."

Pour boiling water over squeezed lemons. Cool briefly; strain and add this infusion to the juices, along with the sugar. Stir to dissolve sugar; taste and adjust sugar if necessary.

Thinly slice remaining halves of each fruit and add to the lemonade. Chill.

Sunny Mimosas

Chilled orange juice
Chilled champagne
Lemon or orange twists

In a well chilled glass pitcher, whisk together equal parts of orange juice and champagne; add twists. Serve immediately in stemmed glasses.

Sangria Blanca

White wine sangria is light and refreshing and is great to serve at barbecue parties, Mexican dinners or when just sitting around the patio on a hot summer day.

Makes about 5 cups

1 bottle (750 mL or 1 L) dry white wine
3/4 cup frozen lemonade concentrate
1 cup (or 1 small, 10-oz./285 mL can) soda water
Sugar to taste
Ice cubes
Lime slices

Stir wine and lemonade concentrate together thoroughly. Add soda and sugar if desired. Pour sangria into long, tall glasses over ice, and garnish each serving with a lime slice.

Spiced Pineapple Juice Punch

Makes 8 cups

Spiced Syrup:

1/2 cup sugar
1 1/2 cups water
4 cinnamon sticks, broken
12 whole cloves

Punch:

Spiced Syrup
1 can (48 oz./1.36 L) pineapple juice
1 1/2 cups orange juice
1/2 cup lemon juice
1 1/2 cups white rum (optional)
Ice cubes

Simmer sugar, water and spices together for 30 minutes. You can put the spices in a cheesecloth bag for easy removal, or strain cooked syrup to remove spices. Chill. (This step can be done several days before serving.) Combine cooled spiced syrup, fruit juices and rum if used; pour over ice cubes. Serve in punch cups or glasses.

Marcie's Spiced Tea Mix

Like coffee, tea contains caffeine, which acts as a stimulant and is often referred to as a "pick-me-up." Tea drinking is a social activity, so why not prepare a batch of spiced tea mix and invite someone in for a "cuppa"?

Makes about 1½ cups dry mix

¾ cup orange flavor crystals
½ cup instant tea (not freeze dried)
½ cup lemon flavored iced tea mix
⅓ - ½ cup sugar
1 tsp. cinnamon
1 tsp. ground cloves

Combine orange crystals, instant tea, iced tea mix, sugar and spices; mix well. Store in a jar with a tight fitting lid. Use two to three teaspoons of mix per cup of boiling water.

Mulled Cider

Hot mulled cider is a welcome drink when you come in from the cold, whether you are young or old.

Makes 8 cups

2 L cider or apple juice
1 orange
1 lemon
12 whole cloves (about 1 teaspoonful)
12 whole allspice (about 1 teaspoonful)
3 - 4 cinnamon sticks, broken
½ tsp. ground nutmeg
2 tbsp. brown sugar

Pour cider into a three- or four-litre microwavable pot. Stud orange and lemon with cloves, then slice fruit and add to cider. Tie allspice and cinnamon sticks in a cheesecloth bag; add spice bag, nutmeg and sugar to cider. Stir to blend. Cook on High power for 12 to 15 minutes, stirring once. Remove spice bag and ladle cider into mugs.

Leftovers may be refrigerated and reheated by the cupful.

SOUPS

Bloody Mary Soup

Unpredictable weather is one of the factors we have to consider when planning meals for summer outings. If you plan to serve only cold foods, you can be sure the weather will be cool and/or rainy. And vice versa.

Bloody Mary Soup can be served either hot or cold. If you plan to serve it chilled, prepare it early in the day. It is a dandy beginning for either a casual or formal meal.

6 - 8 servings

2 tbsp. butter or margarine
1 medium onion, finely chopped
3 stalks celery, finely chopped
1/2 cup celery leaves, chopped (optional)
2 tbsp. tomato paste
1 tbsp. sugar
1 clove garlic, minced
1 can (48 oz./1.36 mL) tomato juice
1/2 tsp. lemon juice
1 - 2 tsp. Worcestershire sauce
1/4 tsp. pepper
1/4 cup vodka (optional)
1 tsp. salt (optional)
Sour cream for garnish

Melt butter and saute onion, celery and celery leaves if used, until onion is translucent. Stir in tomato paste, sugar and garlic. Add tomato juice and simmer for 10 minutes

Add lemon juice, Worcestershire sauce, pepper and vodka if used. Puree soup in blender (in two or three batches) if desired. Reheat to serve hot or chill several hours.

Taste before serving and add salt if desired. Garnish each serving with a dollop of sour cream.

Note: This recipe adapts easily to microwave cooking. Cook onion, celery and leaves with butter on High power until onion is translucent (three to four minutes). Stir in tomato paste, sugar, garlic and tomato juice. Cook on High for eight to 10 minutes; complete as above.

Carrot and Orange Soup

This made-from-scratch soup is as good as it looks.

6 servings

2 tbsp. butter or margarine
2 small onions, finely minced
1 stalk celery, finely minced
4 cups defatted chicken stock
OR 2 cans chicken broth, plus 1 can water
3 1/2 cups finely chopped carrots
1 bouquet garni*
1 tbsp. beurre manie**
3 tbsp. orange juice concentrate
1 - 2 tbsp. whipping cream
Carrot curls or finely shredded carrot (optional)

* You can buy bouquet garni in specialty kitchen or food stores. Or make your own: for a fresh bouquet garni, use sprigs of parsley and/or chervil, thyme and a bay leaf. Tie these inside the halves of a celery stalk. For a dried bouquet garni, place one tablespoon dried parsley and/ or chervil, one-quarter teaspoon each dried thyme and basil, a pinch of dried marjoram and/or tarragon, six peppercorns and a bay leaf in a double thickness of cheesecloth. Tie "bundle" securely.

** Beurre manie is a mixture of equal proportions of softened butter and flour.

Melt butter in a two-litre soup pot; add minced onions and celery and cook until onions are translucent. Add stock, carrots and bouquet garni. Bring mixture to a boil, cover; reduce heat and simmer about one hour. Remove bouquet garni.

Strain soup through a fine sieve, reserving both vegetables and liquid. Puree vegetables; put back into soup pot, with stock. Stir in beurre manie and heat soup to boiling. Cook about two minutes, stirring constantly.

Stir in orange juice concentrate and whipping cream. Heat, but do not boil.

Garnish each serving with a carrot curl or finely shredded carrot, if desired.

Cool Gazpacho

For a frosty look, chill glass serving bowls in the freezer for a few hours before serving. On informal occasions, pour soup from a tall jug into chilled bowls.

8 servings

8 medium tomatoes
1 medium cucumber
1 green pepper
$^1/_2$ cup chopped green onions
1 clove garlic, crushed
$1^1/_2$ tsp. salt
2 tsp. sugar
Freshly ground black pepper
3 tbsp. olive or vegetable oil
3 tbsp. vinegar
3 cups tomato juice
Garnishes: chopped tomatoes, cucumber, green pepper, green onions and croutons

Peel and seed tomatoes. Seed cucumbers and peel if skin is waxy. Seed and remove white membranes from green pepper.

Put tomatoes, cucumber, green pepper, green onions, garlic, salt, sugar, pepper, oil and vinegar into blender or food processor. Blend or puree about one minute, or until mixture is smooth.

Stir tomato juice and pureed vegetables together and chill in covered container in refrigerator at least four hours.

Serve chilled, with chopped tomatoes, green pepper, green onions, cucumber and croutons in separate bowls so guests can garnish their own soup.

Cream of Broccoli Soup

Soup from a can may be easy, but homemade soup is unbeatable. Our mothers were expert soup makers, and they added everything possible to the soup pot rather than throw it out.

Soup lends itself to this style of cooking. A cup of this or that; if it's too thick, add more liquid; if too thin, add another potato. It is easy to see most soup recipes were created, not copied.

4 servings

2 cups chopped fresh broccoli, flowers and stems
1 leek or 2 green onions, white portion only
1 stalk celery, sliced
1 tbsp. butter
1/2 cup water
1 tsp. salt
Pinch cayenne
3 tbsp. uncooked rice
2 cups chicken broth
1/2 cup light cream (10% M.F.)

Place broccoli in a two-litre microwavable bowl. Cover and cook on High power for three minutes. Spoon into blender.

Place leek, celery and butter in same bowl used to cook broccoli. Cover and cook on High for two to three minutes or until onion and celery are tender. Add water, salt, cayenne, rice and one cup broth; cover and cook on High about five minutes. Let stand five minutes. Add this mixture to blender, plus remaining broth; blend until smooth.

Return soup to cooking bowl, stir in cream and heat on 70% power for five to six minutes, or until hot.

Creamy Corn Soup

6 servings

5 ears sweet corn
2 medium onions, chopped
1 green pepper, seeded and chopped
2 - 3 tbsp. butter or margarine
2 cups milk
2 egg yolks
1 cup light cream (10% M.F.)
Salt and pepper to taste

Remove corn kernels from the ears, being careful not to cut or slice too deeply. (Deep slicing will include the tougher part of the kernels which do not tenderize during cooking.) Set kernels aside.

In medium-large soup pot, saute onions and green pepper in butter until onions are translucent. Add corn and saute another three to five minutes, stirring constantly.

Add milk and heat just to boiling. Reduce heat, cover and simmer about 15 minutes.

Puree soup, about $1\frac{1}{2}$ cups at a time, in a blender. Return soup to pot.

In a small pan, whisk egg yolks and cream together. Heat gently, just until mixture comes to a boil. Quickly stir cream mixture into soup. Taste and season with salt and pepper if desired.

Serve with bread sticks or crackers.

Quick Corn Chowder

3 - 4 servings

$^1/_2$ cup finely chopped cooked ham
$^1/_4$ cup chopped onion
1 can (14 oz./398 mL) cream style corn
$^1/_2$ cup milk
Dash freshly ground black pepper

Place ham and onion in one-litre glass measure. Cook on High power for 2 minutes. Add remaining ingredients and stir thoroughly.

Cook soup at medium (50 to 70%) power for five to six minutes, stirring once or twice. OR, if available, insert temperature probe in chowder; set temperature to 155-160 degrees F, and power level to medium. Cook until oven stops. Stir; reset probe and heat longer if necessary.

Note: Soups with milk are cooked at a lower power level than those with a broth base. Milk tends to bubble up more quickly.

Chunky Tomato Soup

5 - 6 servings

1 small onion, chopped finely
2 stalks celery, chopped finely
$^1/_2$ green pepper, chopped finely
1 can (28 oz./796 mL) tomatoes
1 can (10 oz./284 mL) cream of tomato soup
1 can (28 oz./796 mL) water
2 tsp. sugar
1 tsp. Worcestershire sauce

For Microwave: Cook onion, celery and green pepper in two- or three-litre microwavable pot with one to two tablespoons water for about four minutes on High or until vegetables are tender. Stir once. Add tomatoes, soup, water, sugar and Worcestershire sauce; cover and heat on High until soup boils (7 to 8 minutes). Stir; reduce power to 30 to 40% (defrost) and cook, covered, 15 to 20 minutes to blend flavors.

For Stove Top: Combine tomatoes, soup, water, sugar, Worcestershire sauce, onion, celery and green pepper in a deep pot and simmer about one hour or until vegetables are tender.

Curried Apple and Squash Soup

A wonderfully, aromatic and creamy soup from Marbles, an Uptown Waterloo restaurant.

8 servings

1/4 cup butter
2 cups chopped onions
4 - 5 tsp. curry powder
3 cups chicken stock
1 cup apple cider or juice
1 medium (about 2 lb.) butternut squash, peeled
3 apples (Ida Red), not peeled, but core and chop coarsely
Salt and freshly ground black pepper
Fresh lemon thyme for garnish, if available

Melt butter in a large four-litre pot. Add chopped onions and curry powder and saute, uncovered, over medium heat until onions are tender.

Pour in stock and cider, add squash and apples; bring mixture to a boil. Reduce heat, cover and simmer until squash and apples are very tender, about 25 minutes.

Puree soup in batches in a food processor, then press through a food mill or sieve.

Season to taste with salt and pepper. Ladle into warmed soup bowls and garnish with lemon thyme.

Fiddley-Dee Fiddlehead Soup

Fiddleheads are the tightly coiled young fronds of ostrich ferns and are "plucked" when four to eight inches tall. Please note: Only ostrich ferns are safe to eat; unless you have expert training, do not pick ferns, buy them commercially.

For a short time in the spring, most supermarkets across Canada carry delectable, mild-flavored, fresh fiddleheads. Fiddleheads can also be purchased frozen.

Fresh fiddleheads need to be rinsed well to free them of dirt. They need only a minimum of cooking — usually sauteed in a small amount of butter and served with a hollandaise sauce or vinaigrette dressing.

Creamy fiddlehead soup is a superb introduction to a springtime meal.

6 - 8 servings

1½ - 2 cups peeled, cubed potatoes
1 can (10 oz./284 mL) chicken broth plus water to make 2 cups
1 tbsp. butter
1 medium onion, chopped
½ cup finely diced celery
1 small clove garlic, chopped
1 tsp. salt
Pepper to taste
2 cups fiddleheads or 300 g frozen
½ cup cream (10% M.F.)
1½ cups milk

Put potatoes, broth and water in saucepan. Bring to a boil and simmer, covered, 20 minutes.

Meanwhile, melt butter in small skillet and saute onion, celery and garlic until tender. Add to potato mixture and continue cooking until potatoes are done.

Add salt, pepper and fiddleheads to potatoes and cook, covered, until tender. Cool mixture slightly. Remove eight fiddleheads and set aside for garnish.

Process soup in batches, in blender or food processor, until smooth.

Return mixture to saucepan, stir in cream and milk and heat through; do not boil. Ladle into soup bowls and garnish each serving with a fiddlehead.

French Onion Soup

Louis XV of France is credited with creating the "king of soups." Upon returning from a hunting expedition, it is reported, the king found only onions, butter and champagne in the royal cupboards. Louis combined the ingredients and created a soup "fit for kings."

6 servings

4 - 5 medium-large onions
1/4 cup butter
2 tbsp. sugar
2 tbsp. flour
1 tsp. thyme
1 tsp. garlic powder
4 cans (10 oz./284 mL each) condensed consomme
1/2 cup dry white wine
1/4 cup rye whisky
2 tbsp. dried parsley flakes
1 can (10 oz./284 mL) water
3 cups croutons
6 thin slices Mozzarella cheese

Peel onions, cut off root end; slice thinly, from stem end. Melt butter in a heavy, three-litre saucepan; add onions and saute over medium heat about 10 minutes, stirring often to keep onions from burning. Blend in sugar, flour, thyme and garlic powder. Cook this mixture another four to five minutes over low heat, stirring constantly.

Gradually add consomme, wine, whisky, parsley flakes and water. Heat mixture thoroughly but DO NOT BOIL. Reduce heat and simmer about one hour, stirring occasionally.

Cover bottom of each onion soup bowl (oven-proof earthenware) with croutons. Ladle soup into bowls, dividing onions equally among bowls. Carefully layer the top of the soup with very thin slices of Mozzarella cheese. Place bowls in oven at 350 degrees F for approximately 10 minutes, or until the cheese browns lightly and soup is bubbly.

Fresh Asparagus Bisque

Asparagus bisque has the flavor of spring.

4 servings

1 1/2 cups cut-up fresh asparagus stems (save tips)
1/2 onion, minced
3 tbsp. butter or margarine
3 tbsp. flour
2 1/2 cups milk, divided
1 tsp. chicken bouillon mix
Dash dried tarragon leaves, crushed

Place asparagus stems, onion and butter in two-litre microwavable bowl or glass measure. Cover; cook on High three to four minutes or until asparagus is crisp-tender. Stir once during cooking.

Stir in flour and one cup of milk. Cook on High two to three minutes or until mixture boils.

Spoon mixture into blender or food processor. Add remaining milk. Puree until smooth, add chicken bouillon and tarragon and pulse just to blend.

Cook asparagus tips in microwave on High in a separate dish about one minute. Return bisque to two-litre measure, add asparagus tips and reheat soup when ready to serve.

Note: Bisque does not have to be pureed the second time.

Garden-Fresh Minestrone

8 - 10 servings

$^1/_2$ cup thinly sliced celery
$^1/_2$ cup thinly sliced carrots
2 cloves garlic, minced
2 small potatoes, diced (about $^3/_4$ cup)
6 - 8 tomatoes, peeled and quartered
OR 1 can (19 oz./540 mL) tomatoes, quartered (include juice)
1 small zucchini, halved lengthwise and sliced
$^1/_4$ lb. fresh green beans, cut in bite-size pieces
1 can (48 oz./1.36 L) tomato juice
2 - 2$^1/_2$ tbsp. finely snipped fresh basil OR 2 tsp. dried
1 tbsp. dried parsley
100 g (about $^1/_4$ lb.) spaghetti*

*Break spaghetti strands into thirds for easier handling and eating.

Combine all vegetables in a deep, three-litre microwavable pot or bowl. Add tomato juice, basil and parsley. Gently press (uncooked) spaghetti into mixture, being careful not to break it more. Cover and cook on High power seven to 10 minutes, or until liquid boils.

Stir, gently moving spaghetti down into soup. Reduce power to 70% (Medium or Medium-High) and cook, covered, another 15 to 20 minutes, or until vegetables are crisp-tender, stirring once during cooking.

Allow to stand, covered, 15 minutes before serving.

Note: Glass or materials other than microwavable plastic may increase cooking time by five to six minutes.

Soupa Avgolemono

The classic Greek soup is really quick and easy. For anyone on a gluten-free or dairy-free diet, this soup is a nice addition to your recipe collection. Whether on a special diet or not, this is a nice light pre-dinner soup that can be served hot or cold.

4 - 5 servings

4 cups chicken broth
3 - 4 tbsp. converted long-grain rice
½ tsp. salt
¼ tsp. dried dillweed
2 eggs
2 - 3 tbsp. lemon juice
4 thin slices lemon
Paprika

Combine broth, rice, salt and dillweed in large saucepan. Cover and cook for 20 minutes or until rice is tender. Beat eggs until fluffy, then gradually beat in lemon juice. Stir a little hot broth into lemon-egg mixture. Return all to soup and heat, stirring constantly until heated through. Do not let soup boil. Serve immediately or chill. Soup can be served hot or cold.

When ready to serve, reheat soup on low heat, ladle into soup bowls and garnish with a thin slice of lemon and a dash of paprika.

Soup Paysanne

6 - 8 servings

3 tbsp. butter/margarine
1/2 cup diced carrots
1/2 cup diced onion
1 cup thinly sliced celery
6 cups beef stock or water
2 cups fresh/frozen chopped tomatoes
1 cup diced potatoes
Salt and pepper to taste
1 cup finely chopped or shredded cabbage
1 tbsp. snipped fresh parsley

In a large heavy saucepan melt butter; gently saute carrots, onions and celery about five minutes. Add stock, tomatoes and potatoes. Cover pan and simmer (do not boil) 35 minutes.

Add seasonings and cabbage and cook over medium heat another 20 minutes. Ladle into bowls and garnish with parsley.

Vichyssoise

This cold soup was created by chef Louis Diat at the Ritz-Carlton Hotel in New York City, and is considered to be his most famous culinary invention. In the days before air-conditioning, the French-born chef was always looking for dishes to cool his customers on hot, sultry summer days. He recalled the simple leek and potato soup his mother made and how, as a child, he always cooled it by adding milk. He created this same soup, served it cold and named it after a famous spa not far from his hometown.

6 - 8 servings

2 cups peeled, cubed potatoes
3/4 cup leek pieces, white part only*
2 cups chicken broth
1 cup milk
1 tsp. salt
Dash white pepper
1 cup light cream (10% M.F.)
Fresh chives, snipped

*Leeks must be well rinsed to remove sand and grit. Remove and discard green top of leek. Cut white part lengthwise, separate the layers with your fingers as you hold it under running water.

Cook potatoes and leeks in chicken broth until vegetables are very tender. Process vegetables and broth in small amounts in a blender, making sure mixture is very smooth.

Return vegetable mixture to saucepan; whisk in milk, salt, pepper and cream. Cook soup a few minutes over low heat. Do not boil.

Pour soup into a covered container and refrigerate overnight or at least four hours until thoroughly chilled.

Ladle vichyssoise into soup bowls and garnish each with fresh chives or finely snipped tops of green onions.

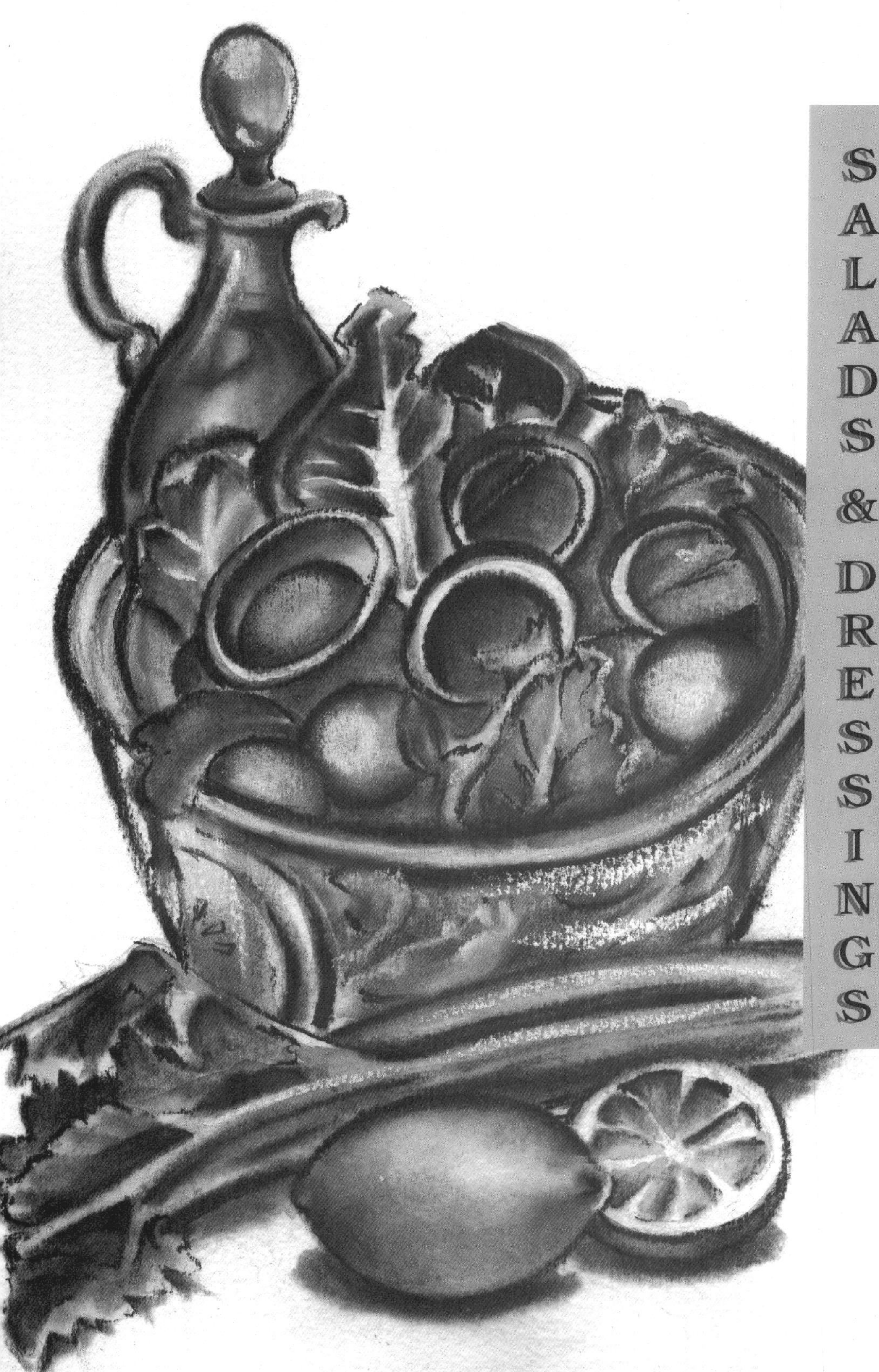
SALADS & DRESSINGS

Audrey's Salad

Be sure to make enough of this delicious salad for second helpings.

8 - 9 servings

Salad:

2 - 3 bunches romaine
1 red onion, sliced in rings
2 cups sliced mushrooms
2 tsp. Salad Supreme*
1/3 cup crumbled blue cheese

Dressing:

1/2 cup peanut oil
3/4 tsp. garlic powder
1 tsp. sugar
1/4 cup red wine vinegar

*You'll find this product with the spices and seasonings in the supermarket, not with the salad dressings. Note that it contains powdered cheese and should be refrigerated after opening.

Salad: Wash, dry and chill romaine.

Just before serving, tear romaine into bite-size pieces and place in a large bowl with onion rings, sliced mushrooms, Salad Supreme and blue cheese.

Dressing: Combine oil, garlic powder, sugar and vinegar in a small jar with a tight-fitting lid. Cover and shake well.

To assemble salad: Pour just enough dressing over the salad to coat, not "float" the greens. Toss well and serve immediately.

Caesar Salad

One of the western world's truly great salads is Caesar salad. It should be eaten immediately after preparation and not allowed to stand at room temperature. Once you have prepared the salad a few times, it is fun to make it right at the dinner table in front of your guests.

8 - 9 servings

1 clove garlic, peeled
2/3 cup olive oil
1 1/2 cups cubed bread, crusts removed
3 heads romaine lettuce
1 clove garlic, halved
1 tsp. salt
1/2 tsp. dry mustard
Freshly ground black pepper
Few drops Worcestershire sauce
1/3 cup red wine vinegar
1 egg
Juice of 1 lemon
3 - 4 tbsp. grated Parmesan cheese

Combine garlic and oil in a glass jar. Cover and let stand overnight. Remove garlic.

Saute cubed bread in three to four tablespoons of garlic oil until toasted. Set aside. If you wish to make the croutons ahead of time, be sure to spread toasted croutons on cookie sheet or plates and allow to cool and dry completely before storage.

Rinse and thoroughly dry romaine; tear into two-inch lengths. Wrap and refrigerate until needed.

Before making salad, assemble all ingredients. Season a large salad bowl by rubbing it with a halved clove of garlic.

Put romaine in seasoned bowl and sprinkle with salt, mustard, pepper and Worcestershire sauce. Gently pour vinegar and remaining garlic oil over salad. Drop raw egg from shell onto ingredients in bowl. Squeeze lemon juice over egg. Toss ingredients lightly until all leaves are coated with dressing.

Top with croutons and toss again. Sprinkle with Parmesan and serve at once.

Greek Salad

8 servings

Dressing (makes about $^2/_3$ cup):

- **2 tbsp. red wine vinegar**
- **$1^1/_2$ tbsp. lemon juice**
- **2 cloves garlic, minced or pressed**
- **$^1/_2$ tsp. salt**
- **1 tsp. dried oregano or 1 tbsp. snipped fresh oregano**
- **$^1/_4$ teaspoon coarsely ground black pepper**
- **$^1/_2$ cup olive oil**

Salad:

- **18 - 30 Greek (Calamata) olives***
- **10 - 12 cups torn lettuce (use some red leaf lettuce if available)**
- **1 red onion, slivered lengthwise**
- **1 green pepper, seeded and slivered**
- **2 tomatoes, chopped**
- **$^1/_2$ - 1 cup crumbled feta cheese**

*If you can't find Calamata olives, use unpitted ripe olives and marinate them in the dressing for several hours.

Prepare dressing first: In a small bowl, mix vinegar, lemon juice, garlic, salt, oregano and pepper. Gradually whisk in oil until ingredients are well blended. Marinate olives in dressing (at room temperature) for 30 minutes.

For salad: Combine lettuce, onion, green pepper and tomatoes in a large bowl. Scoop olives out of dressing and add to vegetables. Drizzle dressing over salad and toss lightly. Add cheese.

Neighbor's 24-Hour Salad

Salads that can be made in advance and just need to be tossed when you are ready to serve, are a great help when entertaining.

8 servings

1 head romaine lettuce
1 - 1½ cups finely sliced caulifowerettes
1 red onion, sliced in rings
6 - 8 slices bacon, cooked crisp, crumbled
½ cup Parmesan cheese
2 tbsp. sugar
1 cup salad dressing

Wash and dry romaine; break into bite-size pieces. Layer romaine in a deep glass or salad bowl; top with all the cauliflower. Continue with a layer of onion, then bacon, Parmesan cheese; sprinkle with sugar. Spread salad dressing over top and right to the edge of the bowl, covering ingredients completely.

Cover bowl tightly with plastic wrap or lid. Refrigerate 24 hours. Toss just before serving.

Tossed Nicoise Salad

Taking liberties with a classic recipe.

6 - 8 servings

4 large potatoes, cooked and sliced
2 cups green beans, cooked
1/2 cooking onion, finely chopped
1/2 cup oil-and-vinegar type dressing OR 1/4 cup each vegetable oil and vinegar
1/2 - 1 cup sliced olives (green or black)
1 stalk celery, sliced
2 cans (7 oz./198 g each) white tuna, drained and broken into chunks
1/2 cup creamy salad dressing (or mayonnaise or creamy Italian dressing)
4 - 5 cups torn lettuce (optional)
2 - 4 hard-cooked eggs, cut in wedges

Combine hot potatoes, green beans and chopped onion in a medium bowl. Pour oil and vinegar dressing over vegetables and toss gently. (Hot vegetables absorb more flavor from the dressing than cold ones do.) Cover and refrigerate for two to three hours.

Add olives, celery, tuna and creamy dressing to chilled vegetables. Toss gently but thoroughly.

If serving immediately, serve salad on lettuce. If preparing salad in advance, omit lettuce, or add it at the last minute. Garnish with hard-cooked egg wedges.

Salad and Lemony Cream Dressing

5 - 6 servings

Salad:

4 - 5 cups mixed salad greens (eg. Bibb, iceberg, romaine and spinach)
1 - 2 cups shredded red cabbage
1/2 cup caulifloweretttes
1/2 cup cucumber (or zucchini) slices, cut in half
1/2 cup chopped green pepper (optional)*
Carrot curls for garnish

Dressing:

1/2 cup sour cream
Grated rind and juice of 1/2 lemon
1 tbsp. sugar
1/4 tsp. seasoned salt
1/4 tsp. celery seed

*Other optional additions or substitutions include sliced fresh mushrooms, alfalfa sprouts, chopped or sliced avocado and/or one-quarter cup chopped green onion.

Salad: Rinse and drain greens and place in a large bowl, add cabbage, cauliflowerettes, cucumber and green pepper. Toss, cover and chill until serving time.

Dressing: In a small bowl, combine sour cream, lemon rind and juice, sugar, seasoned salt and celery seed. Stir until smooth; cover and chill.

To Assemble: At serving time, pour just enough dressing over salad mixture to coat the greens. For tidy tossing "roll" the salad. With spoon in right hand and salad fork in left, go down and forward with spoon as you go up and over with fork. Give the bowl a quarter turn and repeat until salad is well mixed. All the salad remains in the bowl -- not on the counter!

Transfer the salad to a clean serving bowl and garnish with carrot curls.

Sweet and Sour Tossed Salad

6 servings

Salad:

6 - 7 slices side bacon
1/3 cup slivered almonds
Torn lettuce (iceberg and/or romaine)
4 - 5 slices mild onion, separated into rings
1 can (10 oz./284 mL) mandarin oranges, well drained

Dressing:

2 1/2 tbsp. vinegar
3 tbsp. honey
1/4 cup sugar
1 tsp. finely minced onion
1/2 tsp. dry mustard
1/2 tsp. celery seed
1/2 tsp. paprika
1/3 cup vegetable oil

Cook bacon until crisp; reserve two tablespoons fat. Crumble bacon and set aside.

Brown almonds in reserved bacon fat; drain well and cool.

Dressing: In a small saucepan or two-cup glass measure, combine vinegar, honey, sugar, onion, mustard, celery seed and paprika. Stir well; heat just to dissolve sugar. Whisk in oil and set aside to cool slightly.

To assemble salad: In a large salad bowl, combine lettuce, onion rings, crumbled bacon, orange sections and almonds. Pour just enough dressing over salad to lightly coat ingredients. Toss gently and serve immediately.

Spinach-Grapefruit Salad

Popeye visits Sesame Street.

6 - 8 servings

8 - 9 cups spinach, rinsed and chilled
2 - 3 grapefruits (sections and juice)
2 stalks celery, thinly sliced
2 carrots, thinly sliced
Red onion rings
2 hard-cooked eggs, cut into wedges (optional)
Grated Parmesan cheese

Sesame Dressing:

Juice from grapefruit (at least $^{2}/_{3}$ cup)
$^{1}/_{3}$ cup sesame oil
2 - 3 tbsp. toasted sesame seeds
1 tsp. sugar
Dash of seasoned salt and/or dill weed

Tear spinach into bite-sized pieces, combine spinach, grapefruit sections, celery, carrot and onion. Shake or whisk together grapefruit juice, oil, sesame seeds, sugar and seasoning; pour over salad and toss lightly. Arrange salad on plates or bowls, garnish with egg wedges and lightly sprinkle each serving with cheese.

Carrot and Raisin Salad

Young children may wish to help make this salad. If so, they generally are more interested in eating it too!

6 servings

3 large carrots, coarsely grated, about 2 cups
1 stalk celery, sliced
1 unpeeled apple, chopped
$^{1}/_{4}$ cup salted peanuts (optional)
$^{1}/_{4}$ cup raisins
Dash pepper
3 - 4 tbsp. mayonnaise or salad dressing

In mixing bowl, combine carrots, celery, apple, peanuts if used, raisins and pepper. Stir in mayonnaise and mix well. Cover and chill. Brown baggers may wish to pack a serving of salad into individual containers before refrigerating.

Carrot-Green Pepper Salad

8 - 10 servings

2- 3 cups diagonally sliced carrots (6 - 7 medium carrots)
1- 2 onions, coarsely chopped
1 green pepper, coarsely chopped

Dressing:

1 can (10 oz./284 mL) condensed tomato soup
1/2 cup sugar
1/2 cup white vinegar
1/3 cup vegetable oil
1 tsp. Worcestershire sauce
1 tsp. prepared mustard
Salt and pepper to taste

Cook the carrots in a small amount of boiling water, just until they are crisp-tender (about eight minutes). Drain well; place in a bowl and add onion(s) and green pepper. Heat the soup, sugar, vinegar, oil, Worcestershire sauce, mustard, salt and pepper together, but do not boil. Stir dressing and pour over vegetables.

Cover salad and chill for several hours or overnight. Note that it is not necessary to drain the salad before serving.

Carrot-Waldorf Salad

Thanks to controlled atmosphere storage and imported produce, apples and carrots are always "in season".

3 - 4 servings

2 medium carrots, coarsely shredded
1 red apple, cored and chopped
2 green onions, sliced
1/3 cup sliced celery
3 - 4 tbsp. salad dressing or mayonnaise
Dash of seasoned salt
2 tbsp. toasted sunflower seeds or slivered almonds

Combine carrots, apple, onion and celery in a medium size bowl. Add salad dressing, and mix well. Sprinkle with salt and sunflower seeds; toss gently.

Moulded Carrot and Raisin Salad

This salad appears to be rich and creamy, as if made with cream or mayonnaise. The same effect, but not the calorie count, is achieved by beating chilled 2% evaporated milk into partially set gelatin.

Without a doubt, this brightly colored, refreshing salad will perk up winter appetites.

8 servings

1 can (14 oz./398 mL) crushed pineapple
1 package (85 g) orange-flavored gelatin
1 cup very cold 2% evaporated milk
1 cup finely shredded carrot
1/2 cup raisins

Drain pineapple well, reserving juice. If necessary, add water to juice to make two-thirds cup liquid.

Combine liquid and gelatin in a small saucepan or microwavable bowl and heat until gelatin dissolves, stirring frequently. Cool until gelatin is almost set.

With a rotary beater or electric mixer, beat gelatin vigorously until frothy. Gradually beat in cold evaporated milk and continue beating until mixture is light and airy. Fold in pineapple, carrots and raisins.

Rinse a six-cup (1.5-litre) mould with cold water or give it a thin coating of vegetable oil. Put gelatin mixture into prepared mould, cover with plastic wrap and chill until set.

When ready to unmould salad, dip the mould into a dish of hot (not boiling) water for 10 seconds. Run a knife around edge of mould, invert a serving plate over mould and holding both plate and mould firmly, invert.

Emerald Isle Salad

Food writers tend to get real corny around St. Patrick's Day. Even if we can't find a single Irish ancestor in our family tree, we have to serve something green on March 17.

Pleasing to the eye and the palate, this salad has cucumbers arranged to resemble a shamrock in a clear, green top layer. The bottom layer is rich with mayonnaise and evaporated milk and crunchy with vegetables.

6 servings

2 packages (85 g each) lime-flavored gelatin
1/2 tsp. salt
2 cups boiling water, divided
1/4 cup lemon juice
3/4 cup cold water
1/4 cup mayonnaise or salad dressing
2/3 cup evaporated milk
3 thin, cucumber slices
1 small carrot, shredded
1/2 cup shredded cabbage (optional)
1/4 cup finely chopped celery

Dissolve one package gelatin and one-quarter teaspoon salt in one cup boiling water. Add lemon juice and cold water. Chill to consistency of unbeaten egg whites.

Dissolve remaining gelatin and one-quarter teaspoon salt in one cup boiling water. Refrigerate to cool, stirring occasionally. When cool, add mayonnaise and milk. Beat with rotary beater until blended. Chill to consistency of unbeaten egg whites.

Arrange cucumber slices on bottom of a lightly oiled five-cup mould to resemble the leaves of a shamrock. Carefully spoon clear glelatin mixture over cucumber.

Stir carrots, cabbage if used, and celery into remaining, thickened gelatin mixture. Spoon on top of clear gelatin layer. Chill two to three hours, or until firm.

Unmould onto a plate and garnish with parsley if desired.

Orange-Blossom Cauliflower Salad

The dressing accompanying this salad would be sensational on fruit salads too. If you do not need such a large salad, use a small can (160 mL) of evaporated milk and half of a small can of frozen orange juice concentrate (about one-third cup).

12 - 14 servings

Salad:

3 cans (10 oz./284 mL each) mandarin orange segments, drained
4 cups caulifloweretttes
1 green pepper, chopped
2 heads romaine lettuce

Dressing:

1 can (385 mL) evaporated milk
3/4 cup frozen orange juice concentrate, thawed

Salad: Combine oranges, cauliflower, green pepper and torn romaine in a large bowl. Cover and chill until ready to serve.

Dressing: Beat milk and juice together with a whisk until juice is thawed and dressing is well mixed. Cover and refrigerate until serving time.

To assemble salad: When ready to serve, toss about one-half cup of dressing with salad, or put dressing in a pitcher and pass for guests to serve themselves.

Leftover dressing must be kept very cold and mixed well before using.

Crunchy Mandarin Salad

8 - 10 servings

Dressing:

2/3 cup yogurt (tropical fruit flavor or plain)
1 1/2 tbsp. liquid honey
Dash each of salt and lemon pepper

Salad:

2 - 3 stalks celery, sliced
3 medium carrots, coarsely shredded
2 cans (10 oz./284 mL each) mandarin orange segments, well drained
2 large red apples, coarsely chopped*
3/4 cup toasted sliced almonds (or chopped nuts of your choice)
Lettuce

*To keep the apples from discoloring, put them into the syrup from the mandarins, then lift them out with a slotted spoon.

Stir together yogurt, honey, salt and pepper. Set aside (refrigerate if not planning to use right away).

In mixing bowl, combine celery, carrots, mandarins and apples. Stir in a few of the nuts and the dressing.

Line serving bowl with lettuce, add salad and sprinkle remaining nuts on top. Serve immediately.

If you wish to prepare the salad in advance, combine vegetables and fruit with the dressing, but omit the nuts until just before serving. The dressing becomes a little watery during chilling, so lift salad out of the bowl with a slotted spoon; stir in nuts and proceed as above.

Orange Waldorf Salad

Orange Waldorf — a perfect combo to complement roast turkey or pork.

6 - 8 servings

2 oranges
1/8 teaspoon cinnamon
1/2 cup mayonnaise or salad dressing
4 medium red apples, unpeeled
1 cup miniature marshmallows (optional)
1 stalk celery, sliced
1/4 cup nuts (walnuts or pecans) OR slivered toasted almonds OR toasted sunflower seeds
Lettuce (optional)

Grate the rind of one orange. Add rind and cinnamon to mayonnaise, mix well.

Peel both oranges then cut into bite-size pieces. Core apples and cut into bite-size pieces.

Mix fruit with mayonnaise, marshmallows, if used, and celery. Chill until serving time.

Add nuts just before serving. Serve on lettuce if desired.

Composed Peach, Vegetable Salad

A composed salad is just that — the components are carefully arranged, either in concentric circles or like the spokes of a wheel, rather than tossed or mixed together.

This tasty dressing can be used on tossed green salads too.

8 - 10 servings

Dressing:

1/2 cup vegetable oil
1/4 cup basil vinegar (OR use cider vinegar plus 1 tsp. of dried basil)
1/2 tsp. dry mustard
2 tsp. honey or sugar
Freshly ground pepper to taste
Seasoned salt to taste

Salad:

1 bunch leaf or romaine lettuce
500 mL cottage cheese
6 - 7 peaches, sliced*
3 - 4 stalks celery, sliced diagonally
1 green pepper, sliced
1 sweet red pepper, sliced
About 2 cups sliced zucchini
2 - 3 tomatoes, cut in wedges

*Peel peaches if you wish.

Prepare dressing by combining all ingredients in a jar with a tight-fitting lid and shake well. Set aside (or refrigerate until needed). Shake again just before using.

Arrange lettuce leaves on individual serving plates or a large platter. Place cottage cheese in centre.

At "twelve, three, six and nine o'clock" arrange a row of peach slices. Place celery, peppers, zucchini and tomatoes in spaces between peaches (one vegetable per space).

Drizzle dressing over salad and serve immediately.

Simon's Spinach Salad

The bright colors of fresh fruits make this salad appeal to the eye as well as the palate. Salads are made individually like a composed salad and can vary according to your taste or availability of ingredients.

Spinach
Fresh fruit: apples, pears, peaches or nectarines, bananas and/or strawberries
Maple dressing, recipe follows
Pine nuts or cashews

Wash and spin dry spinach; tear into bite-size pieces and place on individual salad plates.

Arrange sliced fruit over spinach. Pour one to two tablespoons of Maple Dressing over each salad and top with nuts.

MAPLE DRESSING

One of the great joys of spring in Ontario is the brief sweet season of the annual maple syrup "crop." It's a special event, for Ontario is one of only a handful of places around the world where maple syrup can be produced.

Makes 1 3/4 cups

1 tbsp. Dijon mustard
1 whole egg
1/8 tsp. salt
1/8 tsp. pepper
1 cup plus 2 tbsp. vegetable oil
3 - 4 tsp. fresh lemon juice
1/4 cup pure maple syrup

Combine mustard, egg, salt and pepper in bowl of electric mixer. With mixer running at medium speed, gradually add oil in a thin but steady stream. Add juice and continue to beat; then with mixer running add syrup and blend thoroughly.

Store dressing in a covered container and refrigerate. Use within one month.

Having all ingredients at room temperature before mixing will produce a greater volume of dressing.

Sweet and Sour Beet Salad

6 - 8 servings

1½ lbs. young, fresh beets, including tops
250 g side bacon
½ cup cider vinegar
2 tsp. sugar
½ tsp. dry mustard
2 tbsp. snipped fresh dill or 1 tsp. dried
About 2 cups garlic-flavored croutons

Trim beets and rinse well; cook until tender in water to cover. Drain, cool and slip off the skins and stems. Cut into one-quarter inch slices.

Meanwhile, wash and spin dry beet greens.

Cook bacon in a skillet until crisp; pour off fat and reserve five to six tablespoons. Drain and crumble bacon.

Put vinegar, sugar and mustard in skillet. Boil, stirring frequently until reduced to about three tablespoons.

Add reserved bacon fat, including the brown "bits". Bring dressing to a boil.

Arrange beet greens on a large platter; put the sliced beets in the centre and surround them with the bacon and croutons. Sprinkle dill over beets and drizzle warm dressing over salad. Serve immediately.

If salad is made ahead, reheat dressing and pour over salad just before serving.

Deli Cole-Slaw

The flavor improves if this salad is prepared and refrigerated several hours or even the day before serving.

8 - 10 servings

6 cups finely shredded cabbage*
1/2 cup mayonnaise OR 1/4 cup each mayonnaise and yogurt
1 tbsp. sugar
1 tbsp. cider vinegar
1/2 tsp. celery seed
1 tsp. seasoned salt
Dash pepper

*If you have a food processor, use the slicing blade to give the proper cut.

In a large bowl, whisk together the mayonnaise, sugar, vinegar, celery seed, salt and pepper. Stir in cabbage; cover tightly and refrigerate for at least two hours.

Refrigerate any leftover salad immediately and use within three to four days.

Sweetened Vinegar Dressing

Makes about 2 cups

1 cup brown sugar
1 cup white vinegar
1 cup water
1/2 tsp. salt

Combine sugar, vinegar, water and salt in a saucepan. Stir until sugar and salt are dissolved. Heat mixture to a simmer; do not boil. Cool dressing and pour into a bottle or cruet. Store in refrigerator.

To use, drizzle dressing over freshly washed and dried leaf lettuce; toss and serve immediately.

MEAT FISH POULTRY

Beef Balls Bourguignon

8 - 10 servings

1 kg (2$^1/_4$ - 2$^1/_2$ lb.) lean ground beef
$^1/_2$ tsp. seasoned salt
$^1/_4$ tsp. freshly ground pepper
1 tbsp. butter or margarine
3 tbsp. brandy or cognac
$^1/_2$ lb. small fresh mushrooms
$^1/_2$ lb. small white (silverskin) onions OR 3 cooking onions, sliced
2 tbsp. all purpose flour
$^1/_2$ cup condensed beef bouillon
1 cup Burgundy or dry red wine
$^1/_2$ cup port
1 tsp. Kitchen Bouquet (optional)
2 tbsp. tomato paste
1 bay leaf

Lightly mix beef with salt and pepper; shape into large meatballs (30 to 40).

Melt butter in Dutch oven or large, heavy skillet and brown meat balls, one layer at a time. As meatballs brown, place them in a casserole or large bowl.

In a one-cup glass measure, heat brandy in microwave just until tiny bubbles form around edge. Ignite and pour over meatballs immediately. When flame dies out, cover meatballs and keep warm.

Add mushrooms to drippings in cooking pot; cook until lightly browned (three to four minutes). Remove and add to meatballs. Cook onions in drippings until lightly browned and beginning to soften. Remove with slotted spoon and add to meatballs. If drippings are very fatty, drain off all but one to two tablespoons.

Stir flour into bouillon and add to pot along with Burgundy, port, Kitchen Bouquet (if used), tomato paste and bay leaf. Cook and stir until sauce is thickened and smooth. Reduce heat, cover and simmer 10 minutes.

Return meatballs and vegetables to pot; stir well. Cover and simmer 30 minutes, stirring once. Discard bay leaf.

Serve hot with crusty bread or rolls.

Gwen's Cheeseburger Pie

Gwen found this recipe a boon in her busy household of six children, two dogs, two cats and a bird. She would precook the ground beef and onion. When one of the young children who was on kitchen duty came home, it was easy for her to complete the recipe and put the pie in the oven to cook.

Makes one 10-inch pie (6 - 8 servings)

.5 kg (1 lb.) lean ground beef
1 - 2 onions, chopped
1 - 2 tbsp. vegetable oil
1/2 tsp. salt
1/4 tsp. pepper
1 1/2 cups milk
3/4 cup biscuit mix
3 eggs
2 tomatoes, sliced
1 cup shredded cheddar cheese

Brown beef and onion in oil. Add salt and pepper; stir well. Lightly grease pie plate then spread beef mixture over bottom.

In blender, combine milk, biscuit mix and eggs; blend for 15 seconds. (If blender is not available, beat with electric mixer on high for one minute.) Pour mixture over meat.

Bake at 400 degrees F for 25 minutes. Pie will be cooked when a knife inserted near centre of pie comes out clean.

Top pie with sliced tomatoes and sprinkle with cheese. Return pie to oven for another five minutes or until cheese is melted. Let stand a few minutes before cutting and serving.

Serve with carrot and celery sticks and rolls.

Italian Meat Pie

6 - 8 servings

Shell:

.65 kg (1 1/2 lb.) medium or lean ground beef
1/2 cup rolled oats
1/2 cup ketchup
1 egg
1/2 tsp. salt
1/8 tsp. pepper
1/8 tsp. garlic powder

Filling:

2 small (6 - 7 inches) zucchini
1 small red onion, sliced
1 cup (113 g) shredded mozzarella cheese, divided
1/2 cup tomato sauce
1/2 tsp. dried oregano, crushed
1/2 tsp. dried basil
2 tbsp. grated Parmesan cheese

Combine ground beef, oats, ketchup, egg, salt, pepper and garlic powder; mix well. Press meat mixture onto bottom and sides of a nine- or 10-inch pie plate, leaving a "hollow" in the centre for the filling.

Bake shell at 350 degree F for 12 minutes. Drain off fat.

Wash zucchini, slice thinly and steam for about four minutes or microwave on High for one to two minutes. (Zucchini should be slightly softened.)

Drain zucchini and mix with onion, one-half cup mozzarella cheese, tomato sauce, oregano and basil; spoon this mixture into meat pie shell. Top with remaining mozzarella cheese and sprinkle with Parmesan cheese.

Bake at 350 degrees F for 20 minutes. Cut into wedges to serve.

Beef Medallions With Wine Sauce

The cost of beef tenderloin makes it prohibitive for serving to a crowd, so save it for a special dinner a deux.

2 servings

.2 - .3 kg (1/2 - 2/3 lb.) beef tenderloin*
2 tbsp. all purpose flour
Vegetable oil
1 stalk celery, chopped
1/4 tsp. fennel seed
2 tbsp. dry red wine
1/4 tsp. beef bouillon concentrate
1/3 cup water

*You may have to purchase a larger piece of tenderloin unless you buy it at a delicatessen.

Slice beef crosswise into half-inch thick slices; place between two sheets of plastic wrap and pound to one-quarter-inch thickness with the flat side of a meat mallet or cleaver. (You can do this early in the day to speed meal preparation.)

Spread flour in a shallow dish; lightly coat both sides of prepared beef with flour, shaking off excess. Reserve the unused flour.

In a large skillet, heat one to two tablespoons oil; add beef and cook just until browned on both sides (three to five minutes). Remove beef and keep warm while preparing sauce.

Add another tablespoon oil to skillet and saute celery and fennel seed until celery is tender; stirring frequently. Stir in one teaspoon of reserved flour, then add wine, bouillon concentrate and water. Cook until sauce is boiling; reduce heat and cover pan. Simmer sauce, stirring occasionally, about five minutes. Serve sauce in a small gravy boat.

Dilled Short Ribs and Carrot Gravy

Two thousand years ago the Etruscans were wrapping food in wet clay and cooking the whole package. Then they broke the dried clay and removed the steamed food! It isn't necessary to break the pot for any of today's clay baker cooking.

This form of cooking is good for the tougher cuts of meat. The pot and lid must be soaked before using. Then during cooking, the water that was absorbed is released and helps to make the meat tender and moist.

If you do not have a clay baker, use a Dutch oven, brown the ribs first in two tablespoons of oil and increase the water to one cup.

6 servings

1.5 kg (3 - 4 lb.) beef short ribs
1 small onion, chopped
1 cup grated carrot
1 tbsp. cider vinegar
1 tsp. salt
1/4 tsp. pepper
1/2 cup water or beef broth
1 - 2 tsp. dried dill weed
1 package (225 g/8 oz.) wide egg noodles OR 6 medium potatoes, boiled
1 tbsp. butter OR olive oil (optional)
2 tbsp. all purpose flour
1/4 cup cold water

Put the ribs, onion, carrot, vinegar, salt, pepper and water or broth in a presoaked clay baker. Cover pot and set it in a cold oven; bake at 325 - 350 degrees F for 1 to 1 1/2 hours.

Ten to fifteen minutes before serving, pour off pan juices. Skim fat from the pan juices and add water if necessary to make two cups liquid.

Cook noodles according to package directions. Drain and toss with one tablespoon butter or olive oil; keep warm.

Pour pan juices into a medium saucepan. Blend flour with cold water and stir into pan juices; cook, stirring constantly until gravy is thickened and smooth.

Arrange noodles (or potatoes) and short ribs on a heated platter; spoon some gravy over ribs and pass remainder in a gravy boat.

Mining Camp Short Ribs

Beef ribs that are marinated, cooked slowly in sauce and then browned on the barbecue are tender and moist inside and brown and crispy on the surface. They remind us of some we ate at the Mining Camp Restaurant, near Goldfield, Arizona.

About 8 servings

1.35 kg (3 lb.) boneless braising beef or beef short ribs*
Herb Marinade (recipe follows)
OR about 1/2 cup of your favorite marinade**
1 cup All Purpose Barbecue Sauce (See page 210)***

* Braising or short ribs are traditionally quite fatty; when boned, much of the fat is also trimmed away.

** When time is limited, Italian dressing makes an easy and acceptable marinade.

*** If using a commercial barbecue sauce, we suggest that you mix one-half cup barbecue sauce with one-half cup beer.

Place ribs in a shallow plastic or glass dish, or strong plastic bag. Pour marinade over meat; cover (or tie bag) and refrigerate for three to six hours. Turn meat over at least once, if possible.

Remove meat from marinade (brushing off the mint sprigs and lemon strips if herb marinade is used). Place meat in a shallow foil pan or small roaster. Pour barbecue sauce over meat and cover pan.

Place pan on barbecue set at low (325 degrees F if your barbecue has a temperature gauge) and with grill at least five inches above coals. Cook for 1 1/2 hours, turning meat over once.

Remove ribs from pan, wiping off excess sauce. Increase heat to medium and lower grill to three or four inches above coals. Barbecue ribs about 15 minutes, or until well browned. Turn ribs over once or twice and baste with sauce during the last few minutes.

HERB MARINADE

3 tbsp. olive oil
3 tbsp. tarragon vinegar
1/2 small onion, thinly sliced
1/2 tsp. garlic salt

1/4 tsp. coarsely ground pepper
1 bay leaf, crumbled (optional)
2 - 3 sprigs fresh mint
2 - 3 strips lemon peel

Combine all ingredients and pour over meat. Cover and let stand several hours in refrigerator. Stir or turn the meat in the marinade at least once. Use with beef or lamb.

Easy Curried Beef

Stick-to-your-ribs fare!

5 - 6 servings

1 onion, sliced and separated into rings
1 1/2 tbsp. vegetable oil
2 tsp. curry powder
.7 kg (1 1/2 lb.) stewing beef (1-inch cubes)
1 cup fresh or canned mushrooms*
1 tomato, diced
1/2 tsp. salt
1 tsp. sugar
1 1/2 cups boiling water
2 tbsp. cornstarch
2 tbsp. cold water

*If the mushrooms are small, leave them whole; otherwise, chop coarsely. Drain canned mushrooms.

In a 10-inch skillet, saute onions in oil, with curry powder. Add stewing beef, mushrooms, tomato, salt and sugar; stir. Reduce heat and stir in the boiling water; cover and simmer gently for 1 1/2 to 2 hours.

Mix cornstarch with cold water and add to beef mixture. Stir until gravy is thickened.

Serve with rice or noodles.

Chunky Chili

6 - 8 servings

.75 kg (1 1/2 lb.) round steak
2 tbsp. vegetable oil
2 onions, sliced lengthwise
2 cloves garlic, crushed
3 tbsp. flour
2 - 3 tbsp. chili powder
1 - 2 tsp. cumin
1 tsp. dried leaf oregano
1/2 tsp. salt
1/2 tsp. cayenne
1/4 tsp. ground cloves
2 tbsp. brown sugar
1 can (28 oz/796 mL) tomatoes
1 can (10 oz/284mL) condensed beef bouillon OR consomme
Dash dried chillies
3 cups water
1 can (14 or 19 oz./398 or 540 mL) kidney beans, drained

Cut meat into one-inch cubes; brown in oil in a Dutch oven. Add onions and garlic, saute until onions are tender.

Mix in flour, chili powder, cumin, oregano, salt, cayenne, cloves and sugar. Cut up tomatoes; add with their juice to pot, along with bouillon, chillies and water. Bring mixture to a boil, reduce heat, cover and simmer 1 1/2 to 2 hours. Stir frequently during cooking. Stir in beans, heat through and serve.

Silver Plated Steak

4 servings

1 tbsp. onion soup mix
1 tsp. sugar
2 tbsp. water
3 tbsp. ketchup or tomato sauce
2 tbsp. vinegar
2 tsp. vegetable oil
1½ tsp. prepared mustard
Dash hot pepper sauce
.7 - 1 kg (1½ - 2 lb.) chuck or blade steak
2 stalks celery, cut in 1-inch pieces
1 tomato, cut in wedges
1 green pepper, seeded and cut in rings

Combine soup mix, sugar, water, ketchup, vinegar, oil, mustard and hot sauce in a small saucepan and heat to boiling. Reduce heat and simmer 10 to 12 minutes. Cool completely.

Pour this marinade over steak in a shallow dish or plastic bag. Let stand at room temperature for two hours, or overnight in the refrigerator, turning steak over once or twice.

Preheat barbecue according to manufacturer's instructions.

Remove steak from marinade, pat dry and brown on both sides on the barbecue.

Tear off three to four feet of heavy duty foil and fold double. Spread about half of the marinade in centre of foil and place steak on top; cover meat with celery, tomato and green pepper and remaining marinade.

Fold foil over meat and vegetables carefully to form a leakproof package. Handle the package carefully so the foil is not punctured or torn.

Cook over medium-low heat on the barbecue for one to 1½ hours, turning once, until the meat is fork tender.

Baked Scotch Eggs

Scotch eggs make a delightfully different lunch, especially for brown baggers.

Makes 8

2 tbsp. snipped fresh parsley
500 g sausage meat
8 hard-cooked eggs, shelled
1/4 cup all purpose flour
2 eggs, beaten
1 1/4 cups finely crushed cheese-flavored crackers

Stir parsley into sausage meat. Use at least two tablespoons of meat per egg. Wrap each egg with meat, being careful to cover all of the egg evenly. Set aside on a plate.

Put flour on a plate, beaten eggs into a shallow bowl and crackers on another plate.

Roll each of meat-covered eggs in flour, then dip in beaten eggs and finally roll each in crumbs.

Arrange eggs on a rack in a shallow pan. Bake at 350 degrees F about 25 to 30 minutes.

Remove baked eggs from pan and allow to cool thoroughly on a wire rack. Scotch eggs will keep up to one week in refrigerator.

Sausage and Cheese Strata

A strata makes brunch easy.

6 servings

500 g sausage meat
8 slices white or whole wheat bread
340 g (3/4 lb.) Swiss or Monterey Jack cheese, grated
4 eggs, lightly beaten
1 1/2 cups milk
1 tsp. Dijon mustard
Pinch of cayenne
1/2 tsp. Worcestershire sauce
3 tbsp. butter or margarine, melted

Brown sausage in a skillet, breaking it up with a fork as it cooks. Drain thoroughly.

Lightly grease a two-litre souffle dish. Remove crusts from bread and cut bread into half-inch cubes. Sprinkle one-third of the cubes into prepared dish. Top with one-third of the cheese, then half of the sausage meat. Add another layer of bread, cheese and remaining sausage. Top with remaining bread, then cheese. Lightly press down ingredients with your hands.

Whisk together eggs, milk, mustard, cayenne and Worcestershire sauce and gently pour over casserole; drizzle top with butter. Cover and refrigerate overnight. Allow to stand at room temperature 30 to 45 minutes before baking.

Place souffle dish into a larger pan and fill outer pan with water so water comes halfway up the baking dish. Bake at 350 degrees F for 45 to 60 minutes or until strata is a golden brown. Let stand a few minutes before serving.

Dressed Pork Tenderloins

Pork tenderloin is as lean or leaner than most meats; it should not be overlooked nor overcooked.

7 - 8 servings

4 pork tenderloins

Dressing:

1 1/2 cups soft bread crumbs
3 tbsp. melted margarine or butter
1/2 cup applesauce
1/4 cup raisins
1/4 tsp. salt
Dash of lemon pepper

Remove any surface fat from tenderloins; slit lengthwise, being careful not to cut through the meat. Spread tenderloins open, cover with wax paper or plastic wrap and pound to an even thickness with a meat mallet. (Most butchers will do this for you; be sure to explain that you want to stuff and roll the tenderloin.)

To make dressing, combine crumbs and margarine; stir in applesauce, raisins, salt and pepper. Divide dressing among tenderloins; spread down centre of each, leaving at least one-half inch of meat around edges. Starting at narrow end, roll up meat and tie each roll with string in two or three places. Close ends with toothpicks or small skewers.

Put just enough water in a small roaster or shallow pan to cover bottom. Place meat rolls on a rack in pan and cover pan.

Bake at 350 degrees F for 30 minutes; remove cover and cook 30 to 40 minutes longer or just until all pinkness is gone.

Remove strings and skewers; cut meat so each slice is a pinwheel of meat and dressing.

Rolled Spareribs

Cooking rolled, stuffed spareribs in water makes the meat tender and moist.

6 servings

4 - 6 ribs per serving (about 2 kg or 4 lb. spareribs)
Garlic powder
Salt and pepper

Stuffing:

1 1/2 cups soft white bread crumbs
3/4 cup finely chopped or grated apple
1/3 cup minced celery
3 tbsp. minced onion
1 - 2 tbsp. snipped parsley
Dash cinnamon
Salt and pepper
1 egg or 1/4 cup water

Cut ribs into either three- or six-rib sections. Large sections need to be cut between the ribs one-half inch deep to permit the ribs to roll.

Toss stuffing ingredients together and moisten with lightly beaten egg or water. Place stuffing in "hollow" side of ribs. Roll up and tie with string or fasten with small skewers. If using small sections, place stuffing on one section, top with another section; tie together with string.

Place stuffed ribs on their ends in a shallow roasting pan; sprinkle with garlic powder, salt and pepper. Slowly add water to come up half the depth of the ribs.

Bake, uncovered, at 350 degrees F for one hour; turn ribs over and bake another hour, or until meat is tender and well browned.

Tourtiere

Marie Hunt contributed this recipe to our newspaper column in 1978; we have never found a better one. You can use your favorite pastry recipe, but this one is particularly suited to meat pies.

6 servings

Pastry:

2 cups all purpose flour
1 tsp. salt
1/2 tsp. baking powder
Pinch of turmeric
1/4 tsp. savory
1/3 cup lard
2/3 cup ice water
1/3 cup butter
1 egg, lightly beaten
1 1/2 tbsp. water

Stir flour, salt, baking powder, turmeric and savory together in a medium bowl. Cut in lard until it is the size of small peas. Add ice water, one tablespoon at a time, until you can form the dough lightly into a soft and pliable ball.

Roll out pastry, dot with about two tablespoons of the butter and roll up like a jelly roll. With the long side of the roll toward you, roll out again. Repeat twice; chill dough several hours.

Roll half of dough to line a nine inch pie plate, or six individual meat pie shells. Roll remaining dough for top crust(s).

Filling:

.45 kg (1 lb.) ground pork OR mixture of pork and veal
1 onion, chopped
2 medium potatoes, peeled and grated
1/4 tsp. garlic powder
1 tsp. salt
1/4 tsp. sage
1/4 tsp. celery salt
1/4 tsp. nutmeg
1 tbsp. snipped fresh parsley OR 1 tsp. dried parsley flakes
1/2 cup water

Combine meat, onion, potatoes, garlic powder, salt, sage, celery salt, nutmeg, parsley and water in a heavy saucepan and cook until no pink color remains; stir frequently to break meat into small pieces. Cover and simmer 25 minutes, stirring occasionally to prevent sticking. Chill; discard surface fat.

Spoon filling into prepared shell(s); top with pastry and pinch edges together to seal. Combine egg and water and brush over top crust. Make slits in top and bake at 400 F for 35 to 40 minutes, or until golden brown. Serve hot with chili sauce.

Cider Baked Ham

Ham is available fully or partially cooked, with bone or boneless, whole, shank or butt portion. A cured pork shoulder is referred to as a "picnic ham." Fully cooked ham can be served as is or heated to an internal temperature of 140 degrees F (about 20 minutes per pound at 300 - 350 degrees F). Cook-before-eating hams should be heated to an internal temperature of 160 degrees F (about 30 - 40 minutes per pound at 300 - 350 degrees F).

8 servings

2 kg (4 lb.) ham or picnic ham
Whole cloves
1 small onion, sliced
2 bay leaves
1 1/4 cups cider or apple juice

Score rind or fat surface of ham in diamond pattern and insert a clove in the centre of each diamond. Place ham in a well-soaked clay baker, large casserole or small roasting pan. Add onion and bay leaves and pour cider over all. Cover pan and bake at 300 degrees F for approximately one hour and 20 minutes for a fully cooked ham, or two hours for a cook-before-eating ham.

Succulent Roast Pigtails

The secret of success for superb roasted pigtails is to simmer the tails and to trim off excess fat prior to roasting in the barbecue sauce. The cooking time is long, but the succulent meat and tangy sauce is worth the effort.

10 to 12 tails

1.6 kg (3½ lb.) pigtails (meaty part, not ends)
1 tsp. salt
2 bay leaves

Place pigtails in a large pot; cover with water, add salt and bay leaves. Bring to boil, cover and simmer about two hours.

Drain off liquid. Using a sharp knife, cut off all the visible fat from pigtails. Place pigtails in a shallow baking dish or roasting pan. Spoon about one cup of barbecue sauce over the pigtails; cover and bake at 300 degrees F 2 to 2 1/2 hours.

BARBECUE SAUCE
Makes 2 cups

2 medium onions, diced
2 tbsp. vegetable oil
1 can (5½ oz./156 mL) tomato paste
½ cup honey or ¼ cup brown sugar plus ¼ cup molasses
½ cup consomme
2 tbsp. Worcestershire sauce
1 tsp. dry mustard
1 tsp. basil
1 tsp. salt
½ cup red wine or red wine vinegar

Saute onions in oil until translucent; add remaining ingredients, except wine. Heat to boiling; lower heat and simmer 15 to 20 minutes. Add red wine or vinegar and heat thoroughly. Spoon over pigtails.

Note: One cup of sauce is sufficient for 10 tails. If you are not using the remainder of the sauce immediately, refrigerate or freeze for future use.

Pork Souvlaki

Kabobs and barbecuing go together. Some barbecues are equipped with kabob skewers, or you can find them with barbecue tools. The skewers can be long or short, thick or thin, or even twisted, and are usually made of metal, although they may have wooden handles or knobs.

7 - 8 servings

1/2 cup dry white wine
1/4 cup vegetable oil
1/2 cup chopped celery
1 sprig fresh basil OR 1 tsp. dried basil
1 green onion
1 clove garlic
1 bay leaf
1 - 1.3 kg (2 1/4 - 3 lb.) fresh pork shoulder or leg, cut into 1-inch cubes

Combine wine, oil, celery, basil, onion, garlic and bay leaf in blender or food processor. Chop or blend on high speed until the vegetables and herbs are very fine.

Pour marinade over pork cubes in a shallow dish or plastic bag. Cover and refrigerate for at least four hours.

Remove pork cubes from marinade and pat dry. Thread meat on skewers, without "crowding" them. (This assures even cooking.)

Barbecue on a well greased grill over medium heat. (If you can't adjust the temperature on your barbecue, raise the cooking grill to six or seven inches above the coals.) Turn kabobs and brush with marinade frequently, for 15 to 20 minutes or until meat is cooked.

Barbecued Spareribs

4 - 5 servings

1.7 - 2 kg (4 lb.) lean spareribs
Water
$^{1}/_{3}$ cup lemon juice
$^{1}/_{2}$ tsp. onion salt
2 - 3 small dried chili peppers
1 stalk celery with top
All Purpose Barbecue Sauce (See page 210)

Cut ribs into serving-size portions if desired; place in a large kettle. Cover with water; add lemon juice, salt, peppers and celery. Bring just to a boil; cover and simmer about one hour or until tender. Drain and pat dry. (Precooked ribs may be stored up to two days in refrigerator if desired.)

To barbecue: place precooked ribs on well-greased grill, about five inches from medium heat. Brown ribs on both sides (eight to 10 minutes per side). Brush ribs with barbecue sauce and grill another five to 10 minutes on each side, basting often.

Barbecued Lamb Chops

6 - 8 servings

2 tbsp. dried mint, crumbled
$^{2}/_{3}$ cup All Purpose Barbecue Sauce (See page 210)
8 shoulder lamb chops (about $^{3}/_{4}$ inch thick)

Thaw chops if necessary; pat dry with paper towels.

Add mint to barbecue sauce and brush on both sides of chops.

Preheat barbecue according to manufacturer's directions; oil grill. For medium chops, barbecue four to five inches from coals, brushing with sauce frequently for about five minutes; turn and cook three to four minutes on second side, basting with sauce frequently. Increase or decrease time as desired.

Braised Lamb Shanks

We are pleased to be able to include a recipe from 20 King Street, a well-known Kitchener restaurant. This is gourmet-style comfort food.

6 servings

6 lamb shanks (2 packages, frozen)
2 tbsp. vegetable oil
Red wine (see method for amount)
2 sprigs fresh rosemary or 2 tsp. dried
5 cloves of garlic, peeled
6 - 8 cooking onions, peeled and halved*
8 - 10 carrots, peeled, cut into 2-inch lengths
Freshly ground black pepper
Beef or brown stock (recipe in Pantry Provisions)

*Cooking onions are also known as yellow onions.

With a very sharp, thin-bladed knife, remove the fell and about one inch of meat from bottom of each shank. Trim fat from meat. Brown meat lightly in oil in large ovenproof pot or roaster.

Add red wine to pot to a depth of one-quarter of an inch. Add rosemary, garlic, onions, carrots, pepper and enough beef or brown stock to cover one-half to three-quarters of the meat. Bring liquid to a boil, cover pan and bake at 350 degrees F for 1½ hours or until meat is tender. Turn meat over once during cooking.

Before serving, remove meat and vegetables from pan. Reduce liquid by boiling if it hasn't thickened during cooking. Place lamb on warmed platter, surround with vegetables and spoon sauce over meat.

Serve with colcannon or parslied potatoes.

Lamb Chops and Apple-Mint Sauce

4 - 5 servings

4 - 5 shoulder or 10 loin lamb chops, about 3/4 inch thick

Marinade:

1/4 cup lemon juice
2 tbsp. vegetable oil
1/2 tsp. salt
1/2 tsp. black pepper
1/2 tsp. paprika
1/2 tsp. dried mint leaves

Apple-Mint Sauce:

3/4 cup smooth apple sauce
1/4 cup mint jelly
1 tsp. lemon juice

Early in day, put chops in shallow glass dish. Combine lemon juice, oil and seasonings and pour over chops. Cover and refrigerate several hours.

Combine applesauce, mint jelly and lemon juice; heat to boiling. Reduce heat and simmer 10 minutes. Serve warm or cold.

Preheat broiler if recommended by manufacturer; place chops on cold broiler rack and broil, five to six inches from heat for six minutes on one side and four minutes after turning, or until cooked to desired doneness.

Serve with Apple-Mint Sauce.

Osso Bucco

4 servings

2 tbsp. olive oil
1 kg (2 1/2 lb.) meaty veal shanks
2 onions
1 carrot
1 stalk celery, cut into 3 or 4 pieces
1 clove garlic, pressed or minced
3/4 cup dry white wine
1/2 cup chicken or beef stock
2 tbsp. tomato paste
2 medium tomatoes, peeled, cored and coarsely chopped OR 1 cup drained canned tomatoes, chopped
Dash salt and pepper
1/2 tsp. dried leaf thyme*
1/2 tsp. dried basil*

Gremolata:

6 - 8 sprigs (leaves only) fresh parsley
Zest of 1 lemon

*When available, use 1 1/2 tablespoons each of finely snipped fresh thyme and basil.

In a large, deep frying pan, heat olive oil. Add veal and brown on all sides. Set meat, upright (to keep the marrow in place) in a two-litre casserole.

Peel onion and carrot and cut into three or four pieces. Coarsely chop the onion in a food processor, then with motor running, add the carrot and celery pieces. When vegetables are finely chopped, gently cook them in the frying pan for three to four minutes. Add garlic and continue cooking until vegetables are tender (another two to three minutes). Stir in wine, stock and tomato paste and heat mixture to boiling, scraping bottom of pan to loosen any browned bits.

Squeeze tomatoes to remove some of the seeds; add tomatoes to the pan. Stir in salt and pepper, thyme and basil. Pour this sauce over veal. Cover casserole and cook at 350 degrees F for about 1 1/2 hours, or until meat is very tender (ready to fall from bones).

If sauce is too thin, spoon off some liquid and boil in a small sauce pan until reduced to about half of volume. Stir back into sauce.

Gremolata: Chop parsley and lemon zest in food processor until very fine. Sprinkle Gremolata over Osso Bucco and serve with rice or pasta and red wine.

Barbecued Swordfish

Swordfish is fine for barbecuing as it has solid texture that keeps it intact during handling. Even though it is not likely to break when you turn it over, use a hinged wire grill basket if you have one; then all servings can be turned at once.

6 - 8 servings

1 - 1.5 kg (2 1/4 - 3 1/4 lb.) swordfish, 3/4 to 1 inch thick

Marinade:

2 tbsp. grated, peeled fresh gingerroot
2 - 3 tbsp. soy sauce
2 - 3 tbsp. lemon juice
1 - 2 tbsp. vegetable oil
2 - 3 tbsp. snipped fresh parsley
1 - 2 tbsp. snipped fresh oregano or 1/2 - 1 tsp. dried
Dash lemon pepper
1/2 cup clam juice* or water

*Frozen clam juice is available in small quantities at some fish markets.

Remove skin from swordfish and cut into desired number of portions. Place in a shallow dish.

Combine marinade ingredients and pour over fish; cover and refrigerate one to two hours, turning fish over once. Let fish stand at room temperature for 15 to 20 minutes, while preheating barbecue on High heat.

Grease grill or wire basket with non-stick cooking spray. Drain the fish well, so it will brown and not just "stew" in the excess moisture; place basket on grill rack three to four inches above hot coals. Cook for 10 to 13 minutes, turning once, or until fish flakes when tested with a fork.

Crab and Mushroom Quiche

Elegant and delicious, this quiche can be made the day before serving so the flavors blend and mellow.

8 servings

10-inch unbaked pastry shell
6 oz. frozen crabmeat, thawed
3/4 cup fresh, sliced mushrooms
1 to 2 tbsp. butter
1 cup shredded Mozzarella cheese
4 eggs
500 mL light cream (10% M.F)
1/2 small onion, chopped finely
1/2 tsp. salt
Dash cayenne
Freshly chopped parsley

Drain crabmeat on paper towels until as dry as possible and sort through for pieces of shell. Break crab into small pieces. Saute mushrooms in butter for a few minutes, then layer pastry shell with crab, mushrooms and cheese.

Whisk eggs together with cream, onion, salt and cayenne; pour over crab and cheese mixture. Sprinkle with parsley.

Bake (in the lower half of the oven but not on the bottom shelf) at 425 degrees F for 15 minutes, reduce temperature to 300 degrees F and bake another 30 minutes or until a knife inserted near centre of quiche comes out clean. Let stand 15 minutes before cutting and serving.

To reheat, place quiche in a 300 degree F oven for 15 to 20 minutes.

Lobster or Ham Crepes

Always sensational, crepes can be made ahead for easy entertaining.

6 servings

Crepe Batter (makes at least 12 crepes):

1 cup all purpose flour
3 eggs
1 1/2 cups milk
1/2 tsp. salt
1 tbsp. melted butter or margarine

Put flour, eggs, milk, salt and butter into blender. Process until smooth.

Heat a small crepe pan until hot (test by sprinkling a few drops of cold water in pan—water will bounce and sputter when pan is ready). Brush pan lightly with butter.

Spread batter very thinly and evenly in pan; rotate pan until a thin film of batter covers the bottom. Cook until top of crepe is set and underside is lightly browned. Turn and brown other side; the second side cooks in less time and never browns as evenly as the first. This side is usually the "inside" of the rolled crepe.

Stack crepes and wrap loosely in a dampened tea towel until ready to be filled.

Filling (for 12 crepes):

1 can (10 oz./284 mL) frozen cooked lobster OR 1 1/2 cups minced cooked ham
1/4 cup butter
2 cups thinly sliced mushrooms
3 tbsp. all purpose flour
1/4 cup finely chopped green or mild onion or shallots
2 cups chicken stock
3 tbsp. dry sherry
250 mL whipping cream (35% M.F.)
2 egg yolks
1/2 tsp. salt

1/4 tsp. pepper
1/8 tsp. nutmeg OR cayenne*
1/2 tsp. dry mustard (optional)*
Pinch thyme
2 tbsp. grated Swiss cheese

*Use nutmeg with lobster, cayenne and mustard with ham.

Thaw and drain lobster and break into small pieces. Place in a bowl.

Heat butter in large, heavy saucepan; add mushrooms and cook gently for two to three minutes. Lift out mushrooms with a slotted spoon and add to lobster or ham.

Sprinkle flour into butter remaining in pan and stir in onions. You may need to add another tablespoon of butter if mixture is too dry. Remove from heat. Whisk in chicken stock. Return pan to moderate heat; heat to boiling, stirring constantly.

Whisk sherry, cream, egg yolks, salt, pepper, nutmeg or cayenne and mustard if used, together. Stir some of the hot mixture into this. Slowly add all of cream mixture to chicken stock in saucepan; cook, stirring constantly until sauce comes to a boil. Remove from heat. Add one cup of sauce to lobster or ham mixture; add thyme. Set aside remaining sauce.

Distribute filling evenly among 12 crepes and roll up each one. Put filled crepes in a buttered, 12-by-8-by-2 inch baking dish. Pour remaining sauce over crepes; sprinkle with cheese.

Cover pan securely with foil; bake, covered, at 350 degrees F about 20 minutes, or until sauce bubbles.

Or, refrigerate and use within two days; bake at 350 degrees F about 35 minutes, or until sauce bubbles.

Marinated Salmon

Midsummer, the summer solstice on or about June 21, is a time to celebrate -- especially in northern countries such as Sweden. Marinated or boiled salmon is a traditional part of those celebrations. Serve with boiled potatoes garnished with freshly snipped dillweed and add a tossed salad for a meal to remember. This recipe also works as hors d'oeuvres, with buttered toast and lemon wedges or a little sauce.

8 - 10 servings

1 kg or more (2 - 3 lb.) fresh salmon*

For every .5 kg (1 lb.) of fish:

2 - 3 tbsp. salt
2 - 3 tbsp. sugar
Coarsely ground pepper
2/3 cup fresh dillweed

*Pick a piece from the middle where fish is thickest. Have fish merchant cut the fish open along its back ridge; remove backbone, but not the skin.

Scrape fish clean with a knife and dry with paper towels. Do not wash. Rub fish (both sides) with salt and sugar. Sprinkle with pepper. Cover the bottom of a shallow glass pan with dill and put one piece of fish on top, skin side down. Cover fish with dill, place other piece of fish on top, skin side up. Place the thick part of the upper fillet on the thin part of the bottom fillet, exactly opposite to the way the pieces were originally joined. Cover with remaining dill. Cover dish and marinate salmon in refrigerator at least 48 hours. Turn over a few times during that time. Marinated salmon will keep in refrigerator for a week.

To serve: separate fillets, scrape off pepper and dill and cut salmon into paper thin slices, sliding knife along skin to separate flesh from skin. This way the fish is skinned before serving. Marinated salmon is often served with a special sauce:

Sauce for Marinated Salmon

1 tbsp. vinegar
2 tbsp. sugar
6 tbsp. Dijon mustard
2/3 cup vegetable oil
2 tbsp. fresh snipped dillweed

Mix vinegar, sugar and mustard. Gradually add oil one drop at a time while whisking (or blending in blender) constantly. Stir in dill. Refrigerate sauce in covered container.

Seafood Casserole

6 servings

2 tbsp. butter or margarine
2 tbsp. all purpose flour
1 cup milk
1/2 cup finely chopped celery
1/4 cup finely chopped onion
2 tbsp. finely chopped green pepper
1/2 tsp. dry mustard
1 tsp. Worcestershire sauce
1 tbsp. lemon juice
1 can (4.25 oz/120g) crab meat, drained
1 can (113 g) small shrimp, drained
1 can (198 g) solid white tuna, drained
1 cup bread crumbs
2 tbsp. melted butter

In a medium saucepan, melt butter and stir in flour. Gradually add milk and stir until sauce is thickened and smooth. Stir in celery, onion, green pepper, dry mustard, Worcestershire sauce and lemon juice. Add crab meat, shrimp and tuna; break up large pieces of crab and tuna as necessary.

Mix all ingredients together gently but thoroughly and pour mixture into a greased 1.5-litre casserole.

Combine bread crumbs and melted butter and sprinkle over casserole. Bake, uncovered, at 400 degrees F for 20 minutes or until casserole is bubbly.

If casserole has been prepared in advance and refrigerated, increase baking time to 40 minutes.

Beef Sandwich Filling

The final "bits" of left-over roast make a satisfying sandwich filling. All ingredients can be combined, chopped and mixed in one step in a food processor.

2 - 3 sandwiches

1 cup roast beef "bits"
1 hard cooked egg, chopped
1/2 - 1 stalk celery, finely chopped
2 sweet pickles, chopped OR 1 tbsp. sweet pickle relish
2 - 3 tbsp. salad dressing or mayonnaise
1/2 tsp. prepared mustard (optional)
1/4 tsp. horseradish (optional)
Dash onion salt
Freshly ground black pepper
1 sprig fresh parsley, snipped

Finely chop or grind meat; add egg, celery, pickle, salad dressing, mustard and horseradish, if desired, salt, pepper and parsley. Mix well.

For lunch carriers: lightly butter bread before making sandwich to prevent filling from soaking into the bread.

Ham-Slaw Sandwich Filling

Makes 6 - 8 sandwiches

2 cups finely diced or ground cooked ham
1 1/2 - 2 cups finely shredded cabbage
1/2 cup diced celery
1/2 green pepper, diced
1 hard cooked egg, chopped
1 - 2 tbsp. prepared mustard
Dash onion salt OR seasoned salt
1/2 - 1 tsp. horseradish
1/3 - 1/2 cup salad dressing or mayonnaise

Combine all ingredients in a large mixing bowl; toss together until well mixed. Cover and chill. Use within five days.

Spread on whole wheat bread, in pita pockets or on Kaiser rolls.

Pita Pocket Chicken Salad

If toting chicken salad to a picnic or to work, chill it thoroughly first and keep it in a good cooler.

6 servings

2 whole chicken breasts, poached
6 peppercorns
1/2 onion, chopped
Few celery leaves
2 tbsp. honey
2 tbsp. minced, peeled gingerroot
3 tbsp. fresh lime juice
1/2 cup mayonnaise
1/4 cup yogurt
1 mango, peeled and chopped
1/2 honeydew melon, cut into small cubes
3 tbsp. snipped fresh mint
Pita breads, cut in half crosswise

To poach chicken: Skin chicken and place in a microwavable pan. Add 2 cups boiling water plus peppercorns, onion and celery leaves. Cover pan and cook at Medium power (70% power) for 10 to 12 minutes, or until no pink remains in thickest part of the chicken. Let stand, covered, five minutes. Remove chicken from broth to cool; debone. (Reserve broth for soup or sauce.)

Stir together honey, gingerroot, lime juice, mayonnaise and yogurt and set aside.

Cut cooked chicken into bite-size pieces and toss with mango and melon; stir in dressing and mint. Cover salad and refrigerate.

Spoon chicken salad into pita pockets just before serving.

Spring Party Sandwich Loaf

This spring party sandwich loaf has complementary fillings combining pleasing textures and tastes in a rainbow of color. When frosted and attractively decorated, the loaf will be the centre of attraction. You may have to order an unsliced sandwich loaf from a bakery.

12 to 14 servings

1 unsliced sandwich loaf, white or whole wheat
1/3 cup butter or margarine, softened

SALMON FILLING (layers one and four):

2 cans (220 g each) red salmon, drained and flaked
2/3 cup sliced pitted olives (black or green)
Salt and pepper to taste
1/3 - 1/2 cup salad dressing

Combine all ingredients and mix well.

HAM FILLING (layer two):

1 1/2 cups ground cooked ham
2 tbsp. sweet pickle relish
1 tbsp. finely chopped onion
Salt and pepper to taste
1/3 cup salad dressing

Combine all ingredients and mix well.

EGG SALAD FILLING (layer three):

6 hard cooked eggs, chopped
2 tbsp. chopped green onions
1 tbsp. chopped pimento (optional)
Salt and pepper to taste
1/4 - 1/3 cup salad dressing

Combine all ingredients and mix well.

FROSTING:

2 packages (250 g each) cream cheese
1/4 cup salad dressing
1/4 cup milk

GARNISH:

Your choice of:
green pepper strips, carrot curls, parsley and/or olives

Remove crusts from bread; cut in five lengthwise slices. Spread one side of each slice with butter. Cover the bottom layer with half of the salmon filling. Cover with second slice of bread and spread it with ham filling. Cover with third slice of bread and spread it with egg filling. Cover with fourth slice of bread and remaining salmon filling. Top with fifth slice of bread.

The sandwich loaf can be prepared to this point, wrapped securely in plastic wrap and refrigerated for several hours, or frozen for one or two days.

To frost and serve: Cream together cheese, salad dressing and milk until well blended. Spread over top, sides and ends of sandwich loaf. Garnish as desired.

Chill loaf at least twenty minutes before serving. Cut loaf into inch thick slices and cut each slice in half.

California Turkey Melt

A colorful open-face sandwich is one way to use up cooked turkey.

2 servings

2 thick slices French bread*
About 4 oz. sliced cooked turkey
1/2 avocado, peeled and sliced
4 slices cooked bacon
About 2 oz. Meunster (or any mild) cheese
2 - 4 tbsp. salsa

*Slice bread on diagonal for attractive, oval shaped slices, three-quarter to one inch thick.

Place bread in microwavable pie plate, or seven-by-11-inch glass baking dish. Top with a layer of turkey, then avocado, bacon and cheese. Cover dish loosely with wax paper and heat on High power one minute, then at 50% (Medium-Low) power for one minute, or until cheese begins to melt.

Top each serving with one to two tablespoons salsa. Recover with wax paper. Heat another 30 to 60 seconds at 50% power.

Hot Swiss Turkey Filling

5 - 6 sandwiches

2 cups coarsely chopped cooked turkey
1 large stalk celery, chopped
110 g (4 oz.) Swiss cheese, chopped
½ cup mayonnaise
1½ tsp. lemon juice
¼ tsp. salt
⅛ tsp. pepper

Put turkey, celery, cheese, mayonnaise, lemon juice, salt and pepper in food processor; mix well.

Spread sandwich filling on rolls or bread. Loosely wrap sandwiches in white paper towels or wax paper and heat on 50% (medium-low) power about 30 seconds per sandwich.

Monte Cristo Sandwiches

2 servings

4 slices buttered bread
2 slices cooked turkey
2 slices Swiss cheese
2 slices cooked ham
1 egg
½ cup milk
Butter or margarine

Make sandwiches, using turkey, cheese and ham. Beat egg and milk together slightly. Dip sandwiches into egg mixture, turning to coat both sides. Fry in melted butter until evenly browned on both sides.

> **Note:** Flat tongs are best for keeping the sandwich intact while turning. If you don't have them, you can tie the sandwich with string.

Camper's Coq au Vin

Like most classic recipes, coq au vin has survived many adaptations. This version calls for canned vegetables making it ideal for vacationers with limited refrigerator storage, as only the chicken would have to be purchased on location or refrigerated until cooking time.

5 - 6 servings

1.3 - 1.7 kg (about 3 lb.) chicken parts
1/4 cup butter or margarine
1 large onion, finely chopped
1 cup dry wine
1/4 tsp. garlic powder
1/2 tsp. pepper
1 tsp. thyme
1 tsp. marjoram
1 can (19 oz./540 mL) potatoes, drained
1 can (10 oz./284 mL) carrots, drained
1 can (10 oz./284 mL) mushrooms, drained

Saute chicken pieces in butter until golden. If using an electric fry-pan, set dial at 325 degrees F.

Add onion and brown lightly. Reduce heat (to 200 degrees F) and add wine; stir to dissolve drippings in pan. Mix in garlic powder, pepper, thyme and marjoram. Cover and simmer for 30 minutes.

Add potatoes, carrots and mushrooms and simmer another 10 minutes. Serve hot with crusty rolls or garlic bread.

Chicken Salad Veronique

4 servings

1 large whole chicken breast (.5 kg)
1 stalk celery, sliced
1 cup halved seedless green grapes
3 tbsp. mayonnaise OR salad dressing
2 tbsp. plain yogurt
1 tsp. lemon juice
1/4 tsp. curry powder
Dash garlic powder
Romaine or spinach leaves
2 - 3 tbsp. toasted slivered almonds

Split chicken breast; remove skin and fat. In a nine-inch microwavable pie plate or similar size dish, arrange chicken with thicker parts toward the outside of dish. Cover loosely with wax paper and cook on High power for five to six minutes, or until no pink shows in the thickest part (test with a sharp knife).

Let chicken stand, covered, until cool enough to handle. Remove bones and cut meat into bite-size cubes.

In medium bowl, combine chicken, celery and grapes. Mix together mayonnaise, yogurt, lemon juice, curry and garlic powders; stir into chicken mixture. Chill.

To serve, arrange lettuce leaves on serving plates; spoon chicken salad over and sprinkle with almonds. Or use as a sandwich filling in pita breads.

Miriam's Chicken Cacciatore

The secret of this recipe is to cook the chicken first, then bone it. Not only is it a very tasty concoction, but very easy to eat.

6 - 8 servings

1.3 - 1.7 kg (3 - 3½ lb.) chicken pieces
2 - 4 tbsp. vegetable oil
1 cup thinly sliced celery
1 green pepper, seeded and diced
1 medium onion, diced
1 can (7½ oz./213 mL) tomato sauce
1 cup ketchup
½ cup tomato juice
2 tbsp. parsley flakes
1 tbsp. sugar
Garlic powder
Salt and pepper

Trim excess fat from chicken.

Heat oil in a large skillet or Dutch oven and brown chicken pieces evenly; cover pan and cook until chicken is tender (15-20 minutes). Remove chicken to a platter to cool. When cooled, remove skin and bones from chicken and cut meat into bite-size pieces.

Add celery, green pepper and onion to pan and saute (in drippings) until vegetables are tender-crisp. Add tomato sauce, ketchup, tomato juice, parsley and sugar; stir in chicken.

Season sauce with garlic powder, salt and pepper. Heat to boiling; reduce heat, cover pan and simmer one to 1½ hours, stirring occasionally.

Spoon over hot pasta or rice.

Honey-Lemon Turkey Wings

Turkey on the barbecue is not as common as steaks, ribs or even chicken, and perhaps that is why it seems special. Great for casual entertaining or family meals, turkey wings are finger-licking good food but they are not intended for elegant occasions.

Turkey wings weigh about one pound each and consist of three parts:

1) the tip -- least meaty part; is sometimes trimmed before packaging;

2) the middle portion;

3) the "drumette" — so called because this portion, closest to the body, resembles a small drumstick in shape, but is white meat.

Two turkey wings might serve four people. For heartier appetites allow one whole wing per person.

2 - 4 servings

2 whole turkey wings
1 cup water

Glaze:

1/3 cup honey
1 tbsp. lemon juice
Grated rind of 1 lemon
2 tsp. prepared mustard
1 tsp. vinegar
Dash Tabasco sauce

Wipe off turkey; cut off and discard tips if desired. Separate each turkey wing into two parts. Place in large frying pan with water.

Bring to a boil; reduce heat and simmer, covered, for two hours. Refrigerate or freeze turkey. If you want to use the turkey broth, chill, remove fat and refrigerate or freeze.

Barbecue precooked turkey (thawed if necessary) about four inches from medium hot coals for about 20 minutes, turning occasionally to brown evenly.

Glaze: Combine honey, lemon juice and rind, mustard, vinegar and Tabasco. Brush on turkey and cook 10 minutes longer, turning and brushing at least once.

Sausage-Apple Stuffing for Turkey

Thanksgiving and turkey go together like apple pie and cheese. We can vary the tradition by changing the stuffing and this may please both the traditionalists and the innovators in the family.

For a 5 kg/11 lb. turkey

250 g (1/2 lb.) sausage meat
1 stalk celery, including leaves, sliced
1 small onion, sliced
1 cooking apple, chopped
7 - 8 cups soft bread crumbs
1/2 tsp. salt
1/4 tsp. pepper
1 1/2 tsp. poultry seasoning* OR 1 tsp. sage and/or savory
1/4 - 1/2 cup apple juice or milk

*If you like a well-seasoned stuffing, you should be able to smell the poultry seasoning in the uncooked dressing. Take into consideration the amount of seasoning in the sausage meat.

Cook sausage slowly, with celery and onion, until meat loses its pink color and the vegetables are soft, but not brown. Drain off fat.

In a large bowl, combine apple, bread crumbs, salt, pepper and poultry seasoning. Add sausage mixture to crumbs and combine thoroughly. Stir in liquid until dressing mixture is lightly moistened, but not soggy.

Pack dressing lightly into body and neck cavities (it will expand as it cooks). Pull neck skin over opening and hold it in place by folding wing tips over back; or if skin is short, use a skewer to hold it flat. Cross legs and tie to tail with a long piece of clean cord; cross cord at bottom end of breast bone and draw up between thighs and breast to the wings. Turn turkey over and tie cord over wings at the back.

Roasting instructions, including time, will usually be given on the label or giblet bag.

Note: A meat thermometer is the most accurate guide to doneness. It should be inserted into the middle of the thick thigh muscle, parallel to bone and next to body, or into the thickest breast muscle. When cooked, the temperature will be 185-190 degrees F. A thermometer inserted into stuffing should read 165 degrees F.

Wild Rice Stuffing for Turkey

Sufficient for a 4.5 - 5 kg (10 - 11 lb.) turkey

1 cup wild rice
1/4 cup butter or margarine
1/3 cup finely chopped onion
1/3 cup chopped celery
1/2 cup chopped green pepper
1 cup turkey OR chicken broth
3 cups plain croutons
1 apple, peeled and chopped
1 tbsp. snipped fresh parsley
Dash pepper
3/4 tsp. poultry seasoning
1 egg, slightly beaten

Cook rice according to package directions.

Melt butter in a large, three-litre microwavable casserole, on High power, about 1 minute. Stir in onion, celery and green pepper; cook on High for three minutes or until onion is translucent, stirring once. Add broth, croutons, apple, parsley, pepper and poultry seasoning. Mix in cooked rice and egg. Spoon dressing into prepared turkey cavities. Using skewers or string, fasten both openings to hold stuffing firmly in place.

Microwave Bread Stuffing

8 - 10 servings

1/2 cup butter or margarine
2/3 cup chopped onion
1 1/4 cups sliced mushrooms (optional)
1 1/4 cups chopped celery
6 - 7 cups bread cubes*
1 tsp. dried parsley flakes
1/2 tsp. salt
1/4 tsp. sage
1/4 tsp. poultry seasoning
1/8 tsp. pepper
1/3 cup broth or stock

*For best results, use bread that is two or three days old.

Measure butter into a two-litre microwavable casserole; melt on High power for 30 seconds. Stir in onion, mushrooms and celery. Cover and cook on High power for four minutes.

Stir in bread cubes, parsley, salt, sage, poultry seasoning and pepper. Drizzle broth over mixture and toss lightly. Cover and cook at 50% (Medium-Low) power for eight to nine minutes. Let stand 10 minutes before serving.

Good-bye Turkey

A classy casserole from left-over turkey.

5 - 6 servings

3/4 lb. broccoli, cut into bite-size pieces*
7 - 8 slices cooked turkey
2 tbsp. butter or margarine
1/4 cup all purpose flour
1 1/2 cups turkey broth
1 cup dry white wine
1/4 tsp. oregano
Salt and pepper to taste
1/3 cup grated Cheddar cheese
Paprika

*Fresh or frozen broccoli, asparagus, green beans, or carrots, sliced or cut in julienne strips may be used in this recipe.

Cook broccoli until barely tender, in lightly salted, boiling water or by microwave. Drain and arrange evenly in a shallow 2- to 2.5-litre baking dish or casserole.

Arrange sliced turkey over broccoli.

Melt butter in a medium saucepan; blend in flour and let mixture bubble. Add broth gradually, stirring constantly until sauce is smooth and thick. Stir in wine, oregano, salt and pepper. Pour sauce evenly over turkey, sprinkle grated cheese over top and dust lightly with paprika.

Bake at 375 degrees F for 15 to 20 minutes or until hot and bubbly and cheese is melted.

Turkey Curry

Curry powder should not be added dry to sauces, but first cooked in butter or oil to eliminate its raw taste.

6 - 8 servings

2 - 3 tbsp. butter or margarine
1 onion, chopped
1 clove garlic, pressed or minced
1 cup sliced mushrooms
1½ tbsp. curry powder
¼ cup all purpose flour
½ tsp. cumin
1 can (385 mL) 2% evaporated milk
1 cup water mixed with 1 tsp. chicken bouillon concentrate OR 1 cup turkey broth and ½ tsp. salt
4 - 5 cups cubed, cooked turkey

Melt butter in a large saucepan; saute onion, garlic, mushrooms and curry powder until onion is tender. Blend in flour and cumin. Gradually stir in evaporated milk, water/bouillon mixture or broth and salt.

Cook, stirring constantly, over medium heat until sauce boils and thickens. Stir in cooked turkey and cook gently until heated through.

Turkey Burgers

4 servings

1 egg, slightly beaten
1½ tsp. prepared mustard
2 tsp. lemon juice
¼ tsp. powdered sage
.5 kg (1 lb.) ground raw turkey
½ cup soft bread crumbs
2 green onions, chopped
Chinese plum sauce

Combine the egg, mustard, lemon juice and sage in a medium-size bowl; blend together with a whisk or fork. Stir in the meat, crumbs and onions and mix with a fork until well blended.

Moisten hands and shape meat mixture into four patties. Barbecue on a greased grill over low to medium coals for eight to nine minutes per side. Brush both sides of patties with plum sauce at least once during cooking.

Serve on buns or with Rye Herb Bread (See page 202).

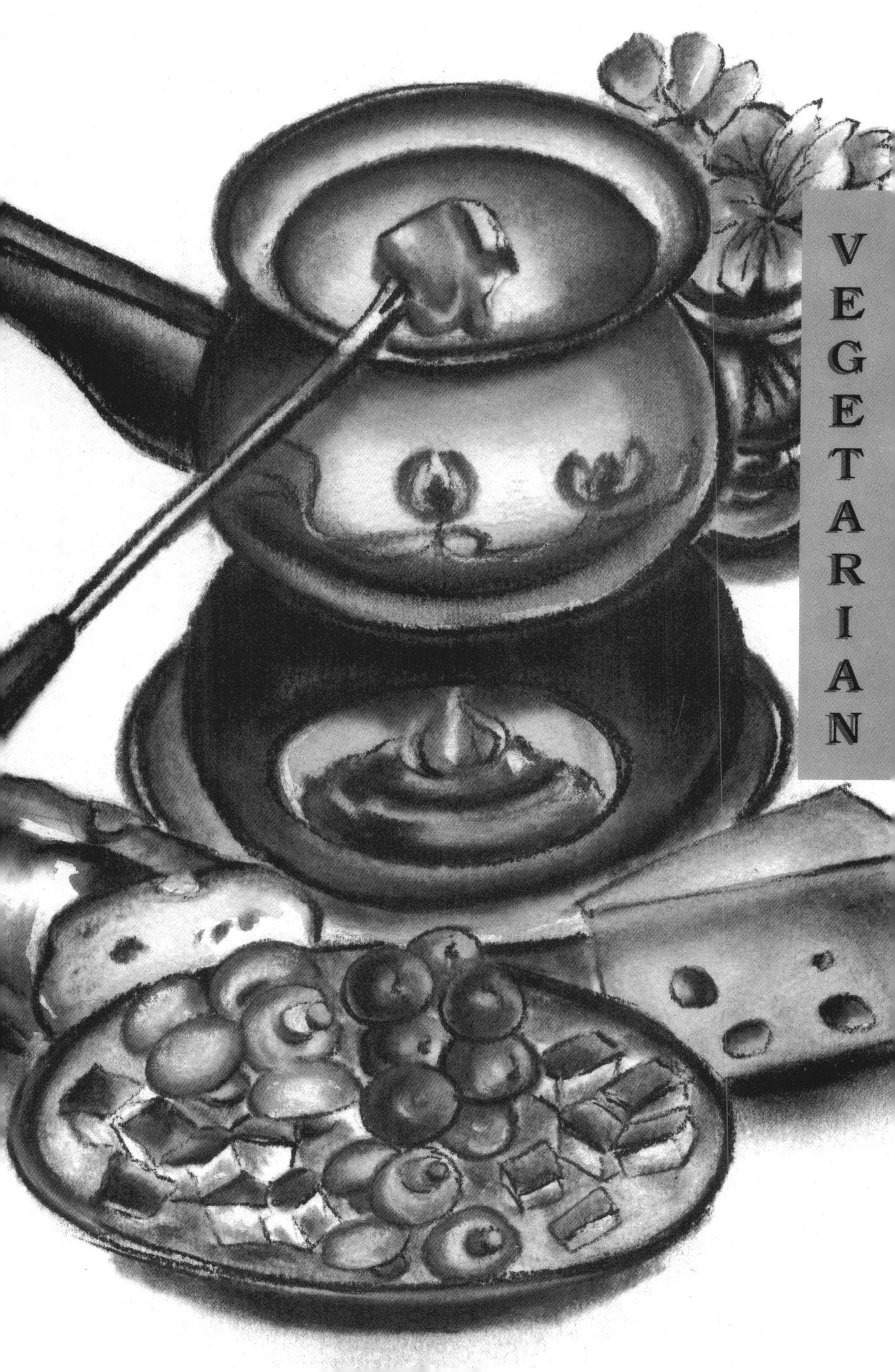
VEGETARIAN

Cheese Fondue

The late Simon Wicki of Waterloo shared his recipe for a Swiss fondue with us.

2 - 4 servings

1 French stick (baguette) cut in cubes with crust on each piece
150 g Emmenthaler cheese
150 g Gruyere cheese
1 clove garlic
3/4 - 1 cup dry white wine
White pepper (about 1/4 tsp.)
Ground nutmeg (about 1/4 tsp.)
2 tbsp. Kirsch
1 tbsp. cornstarch

Prepare baguette and place cubes in a basket lined with a serviette.

Shred cheeses coarsely.

Mince garlic; rub heavy enamelled fondue pot (see note) with garlic and leave remaining bits in pot. Put cheese in pot and add wine.

Place pot over medium-high heat. Stir constantly, in figure-eight pattern, until cheese is melted. Remove from heat. Add pepper and nutmeg. Mix kirsch with cornstarch. Stir into cheese mixture. Return to heat; bring mixture just to a boil.

Pour mixture into fondue pot if necessary (see note) and serve immediately with bread.

Crudities such as broccoli, cauliflower and carrots may also be served with fondue. Whatever you choose, be sure to place it securely on fondue fork. Don't just "dip" into the pot — with each bite, plunge your fork to the bottom of the pot and stir so cheese will not bake on to the bottom.

Note: If you do not have a fondue pot that can be placed on direct heat from a stove, use a heavy sauce pan and, when cooked, pour mixture into fondue pot.

Cheesy Cauliflower-Broccoli Tart

Health professionals tell us that we should befriend "the coles." The cabbage or mustard family of vegetables (sometimes referred to as cole crops) includes broccoli, Brussels sprouts, cabbage, cauliflower, kohlrabi, kale and rutabaga and are thought to contain natural inhibitors that reduce the incidence of some types of cancer.

A prebaked and cooled pie shell forms the base of a quick main dish. This tart (or is it a salad?) is best served at room temperature.

4 - 6 servings

1 baked and cooled 8½ or 9-inch pastry shell
1 cup each broccoli and cauliflower florets
1 cup cottage or ricotta cheese*
¼ cup light mayonnaise
1 tsp. Dijon mustard
Dash of hot pepper sauce
2 green onions, sliced
4 slices bacon, cooked and crumbled
1 - 2 tbsp. Italian or French vinaigrette

*Some of each gives the best consistency.

Place the broccoli and cauliflower in a one-litre microwavable casserole; cover and cook on High power for two minutes. (Or blanch in boiling water for three minutes.)

Refresh vegetables under cold water; drain well and pat dry.

Beat together cheese(s), mayonnaise, mustard and hot pepper sauce until smooth; stir in onions. Spread cheese mixture evenly over pie crust. Arrange broccoli and cauliflower over top and gently press them into the cheese mixture.

Sprinkle bacon over vegetables and drizzle vinaigrette over all.

Serve at room temperature.

Calico Cheese Salad

Add variety to this salad each time you make it by using different dressings. Sweet and tangy vinaigrette, Italian and French dressings are all suitable.

4 - 5 servings

1 can (14 oz/398 mL) red kidney beans, rinsed and drained
1 can (12 oz./355 mL) whole kernel corn, drained OR $1^1/_2$ cups cooked corn
1 cup sliced celery
125 g Cheddar cheese, cut into $^1/_2$ inch cubes (about 1 cup)
$^1/_2$ cup oil and vinegar type dressing
Lettuce leaves (optional)

In a medium bowl, toss the kidney beans, corn, celery and cheese with dressing. Cover and chill at least three hours to blend flavors; stir several times. Drain salad; reserve dressing in case there are leftovers. (The salad will keep for two to three days in the refrigerator.) Serve in lettuce lined bowl if desired.

Rotini With Tomato-Bean Sauce

7 - 8 servings

2 cans (19 oz./540 mL each) tomatoes
2 medium onions, chopped
2 cloves garlic, minced or pressed
1 cup chopped green pepper or celery
$1^1/_2$ tsp. dried basil
$^3/_4$ tsp. dried oregano
$^1/_4$ tsp. salt
4 - 5 cups rotini or fusili (corkscrew) pasta
2 cans (14 oz./398 mL each) beans in tomato sauce
$^1/_4$ cup grated Parmesan cheese

In large pot, mash tomatoes or break apart with a fork. Add onion, garlic, green pepper, basil, oregano and salt. Bring to a boil, reduce heat and simmer, uncovered, for 20 to 30 minutes or until sauce is thickened; stir occasionally.

Meanwhile, cook pasta in rapidly boiling water until al dente. Drain well. Stir beans into tomato sauce and heat through. Divide pasta among serving plates; top with sauce and sprinkle with Parmesan cheese.

Chunky Egg Salad With Vegetables

6 - 8 servings

3 tbsp. plain yogurt
3 tbsp. mayonnaise
2 tsp. prepared mustard
2 tbsp. snipped fresh chives OR 2 tsp. dried chives
1/2 tsp. seasoned salt
8 hard cooked eggs
1 cup diced celery
1 cup finely chopped zucchini
Dash white pepper

Combine yogurt, mayonnaise, mustard, chives and salt in a medium bowl. Coarsely chop eggs and add to dressing, or cut eggs into two or three pieces and use a pastry blender to chop eggs and mix into dressing. Add celery, zucchini and pepper and mix lightly; cover and chill.

Use as sandwich filling or serve in lettuce cups.

Scrambled Eggs With Cream Cheese

4 servings

7 - 8 eggs
1/4 cup water or milk
1/4 tsp. salt
Dash pepper
1 1/2 tbsp. butter or margarine
125 g cream cheese, cut into 1/2-inch cubes
1 tbsp. snipped chives or 1 tsp. dried chives

Beat eggs, water, salt and pepper together until thoroughly mixed.

In a two-litre microwavable casserole, melt butter or margarine on High power for 30 seconds. Pour in egg mixture. Cook on High for three minutes. Stir after two minutes. Reduce power to 70% (Medium-High) and cook another one to two minutes. Eggs should still be moist. Add cheese and stir to distribute evenly. Cook at 70% power for another 20-30 seconds.

Sprinkle with chives and serve immediately.

Tabouli

Tabouli is a Lebanese appetizer or main dish salad that can be served on lettuce, or scooped up with pieces of pita bread.

6 servings

1 1/2 cups boiling water
1 cup uncooked bulgur*
1 tsp. salt
1/4 cup lemon juice (preferably fresh)
1/4 cup olive oil
1 clove garlic, pressed or finely minced
2 tbsp. snipped fresh mint or 1 tsp. dried mint
4 green onions, sliced
2 tomatoes, diced
1/2 green pepper, diced
1 cup snipped fresh parsley
Freshly ground pepper to taste

Optional additions:

1/2 cup cooked garbanzo or navy beans
1 carrot, shredded
1 small cucumber or zucchini, diced

Optional garnishes:

Lettuce
Crumbled feta cheese
Sliced olives

*Bulger is available in natural food stores.

Pour boiling water over bulgur; stir in salt. Cover and let stand 20 minutes, or until bulgur is softened and "chewable." Drain off excess water.

Whisk together lemon juice, oil, garlic and mint; add to bulgur and mix thoroughly. Cover and chill at least three hours.

Just before serving, stir onions, tomatoes, green pepper, parsley and ground pepper into bulgur mixture. Add other vegetables, or garnish as desired.

Vegetarian Chili

Chili without carne (meat) is high in fibre, low in fat and with the combination of bulgur and beans, it is a source of complete protein. This meatless version of chili is thick and hearty, thanks to the bulgur, which expands on cooking. If cooked on top of the stove, use a heavy saucepan and stir frequently to prevent scorching. We have heard that both meat-eating and vegetarian university students love this chili. It is very inexpensive and tastes good too.

7 - 8 servings

1 onion, chopped
1 clove garlic, minced or pressed
1/2 tbsp. vegetable oil
1 can (28 oz./796 mL) tomatoes, undrained
1/2 cup fine bulgur*
1 1/2 - 2 tbsp. chili powder
1 can (14 oz./398 mL) kidney beans
1 can (19 oz./540 mL) chick peas, drained
1 can (7 1/2 oz./213 mL) tomato sauce
1 tsp. dried basil
Dash Tabasco sauce

*Bulgur is available in natural food stores.

In a large (three-litre) microwavable casserole, cook onion and garlic in oil until softened, about two minutes on High power. Stir.

Add tomatoes (break up with a spoon or fork), bulgur and chili powder. Cover casserole with a vented lid and cook on High for eight to 10 minutes; stir once after four or five minutes.

Stir in kidney beans (drained or not, as you prefer), chick peas, tomato sauce, basil and Tabasco.

Cover and cook at 50% power (Medium-Low) for 15 to 20 minutes. Stir after 10 minutes.

Let stand, covered, for eight to 10 minutes.

VEGETABLES

Braised Red Cabbage

This version of braised red cabbage is milder in flavor than similar recipes that use red wine and/or red wine vinegar. It is still a hearty vegetable to serve with hearty meats.

6 - 8 servings

2 - 3 cooking onions, sliced
1 small red cabbage (about 1 kg) shredded, not grated
3 - 4 tart apples
1 tbsp. bacon fat or butter
2 bay leaves
3 or 4 whole cloves
1½ tsp. sugar
1 tsp. salt
1 - 2 tbsp. vinegar
½ cup water

In a large three- or four-quart stainless steel or enamel pot, place onions, cabbage and apples. Add fat, bay leaves, cloves, sugar, salt, vinegar and water. Cook over moderate heat until liquid boils; cover and simmer for about one hour or until cabbage is tender. Stir several times during cooking.

This can be prepared a day or two before serving and reheated.

Saucy Brussels Sprouts

8 servings

.7 kg (1 1/2 lb.) fresh Brussels sprouts
1/2 cup chopped onion
2 tbsp. butter
1 tbsp. flour
2 tsp. brown sugar
1/4 tsp. seasoned salt
1/4 tsp. dry mustard
1/2 cup milk
3/4 cup sour cream
1 tbsp. snipped parsley, for garnish

Wash sprouts well; trim stems and outer leaves if necessary. Make a crosswise cut in base of each.

Cook sprouts just until tender: boil (in one cup water) or steam for 10 to 12 minutes; microwave (no water added) for six to seven minutes; or pressure cook (one-quarter cup water) for 1 1/2 minutes at 15 pounds pressure.

Meanwhile, saute onion in butter until softened, but not brown. Stir in flour, sugar, salt and mustard; cook until the mixture bubbles. Add milk, cook and stir until the sauce thickens. Blend in sour cream and heat through but do not boil.

Drain sprouts well and add to sauce; stir gently to combine. Place in serving dish and sprinkle with parsley.

French Peas a la Microwave

8 servings

2 tbsp. butter or margarine
12 - 16 tiny onions OR 1 cup sliced onion
8 - 10 lettuce leaves, coarsely shredded
2 packages (350 g each) frozen peas
1 tsp. sugar
Pinch of thyme AND/OR basil
Salt and pepper to taste

Melt butter in a two-litre microwavable casserole on High power for 40 seconds. Stir in onions; cook on High for two to three minutes or until tender-crisp. Add peas, sugar and herbs; top with lettuce.

Cover and cook on High for four minutes. Stir, cover and cook another three to four minutes or until peas are cooked and lettuce is limp. Season to taste.

Colcannon

Children, who love special days, may want to help you prepare this traditional Irish dish, sometimes called potato and cabbage pudding. And they may like to eat it the way an Irish expatriate remembers: "Take colcannon on a fork from the outside of the heap and dip it into the centre butter before eating."

6 servings

4 - 5 potatoes, peeled
1/2 tsp. salt (optional)
2 cups finely chopped cabbage
2 tbsp. butter
3 - 4 tbsp. milk or light cream
1 small onion, finely chopped
Salt and pepper to taste
About 3 tbsp. butter, melted (optional)
3 slices bacon, cooked and crumbled (optional)

Boil potatoes in lightly salted water until tender (about 25 minutes). Drain well and place in a mixing bowl.

Meanwhile, chop cabbage (in a food processor if you have one) and cook in boiling water until tender (five to eight minutes). Drain well.

Mash or whip potatoes; beat in two tablespoons butter and enough milk to make mixture light and fluffy. Beat in cooked cabbage and chopped onion. Season with salt and pepper.

There are two ways to serve colcannon:

Place a portion of hot vegetable mixture on each plate. With the back of a spoon, make a well in the top. Pour some melted butter into each well and eat as suggested above.

Or put potato-cabbage mixture in a greased 1.5-litre casserole. If vegetables have cooled, bake at 400 degrees F until heated through. Top with crumbled bacon if desired.

Duchesse Potatoes

2 - 3 servings

2 cups mashed potatoes
1 whole egg
1/4 cup grated cheese (optional)
Paprika

Add egg and cheese to hot mashed potatoes. Beat until light. Spoon mixture into lightly greased one-litre casserole and sprinkle with paprika.

Bake at 425 degrees F for 20minutes.

Potato Pancakes

A food processor permits speedy, easy mixing and grating just by changing blades.

6 servings

Bacon fat or oil for frying
1/3 cup all purpose flour
1/2 tsp. salt
Dash pepper
3/4 tsp. baking powder
3 eggs
1/8 onion
4 large potatoes, peeled

Heat a heavy frypan, add just enough fat to lightly grease it. (Pan will be hot enough when a drop of water will sizzle.)

Combine flour, salt, pepper and baking powder in food processor. Pulse to mix; add eggs and onion. Process until well blended and onion is finely chopped. Remove cutting blade and put shredder in place. Add potatoes, process. Remove shredder and stir potatoes into batter. (If a food processor is not available, simply chop onions finely and shred potatoes by hand before mixing.)

Drop about one-third cup batter per pancake onto hot pan. Flatten if necessary, and cook until crisp and brown on both sides (about four to five minutes on each side). Serve immediately.

Note: Most recipes for potato pancakes suggest serving them with sour cream or applesauce, but for a real Waterloo County flair, spread with apple butter.

Savory Potato Wedges

4 - 5 servings

4 - 5 medium potatoes*
Boiling water
2 tbsp. lemon juice
1 clove garlic, minced or crushed
4 green onions, sliced
1½ tbsp. margarine or butter
Grated rind of ½ lemon
½ tsp. dried dill weed
¼ tsp. seasoned salt

*We like to use unpeeled red potatoes

Cut each potato into six or eight wedges. Cook wedges in boiling water with lemon juice and garlic until tender, about 20 minutes; drain well. Set potatoes aside. In same pan, saute onions in margarine. Add potatoes, lemon rind, dill weed and salt; toss gently. Heat through.

Scalloped Potatoes

Scalloped potatoes are especially good with meats that do not have their own gravy or sauce, such as ham, sausages and cold meats. They are also a good accompaniment for spareribs and pigtails and are sometimes the only hot food served at an informal buffet meal.

6 - 8 servings

3 tbsp. butter or margarine
3 tbsp. flour
½ tsp. salt
¼ tsp. white pepper
2¼ cups milk
5 - 6 cups thinly sliced potatoes
1 small onion, thinly sliced (optional)

Melt butter over low heat; stir in flour, salt and pepper until well blended. Let mixture cook until it bubbles. Gradually add milk, stirring constantly until sauce is smooth and thick and there is no taste of uncooked flour.

Meanwhile, arrange potato and onion slices in alternate layers in a three-litre greased casserole. Pour sauce over vegetables. Bake uncovered at 350 degrees F for one hour or until potatoes are tender.

On the grill

Advance planning and preparation adds variety to outdoor meals. Here are a couple of delicious options.

SKEWERED POTATOES AND ONIONS

This recipe is easily adjusted to any number of servings.

New, red skinned potatoes, scrubbed, not peeled*
Small onions, peeled
Butter or vegetable oil
Barbecue spice or seasoned salt

*If tiny potatoes are not available, cut potatoes into halves or quarters.

Early in the day, cook potatoes in boiling water about five minutes. Add onions and cook five minutes longer. Drain; chill under cold running water. Drain well and pat dry. Cover and refrigerate until ready to finish cooking.

Shortly before serving, heat butter in a skillet; add vegetables and toss gently to coat. Sprinkle with seasoning and thread onto oiled skewers.

Grill, turning frequently, for six to eight minutes, or until heated through.

GRILLED ONIONS AND ORANGES

4 - 5 servings

2 - 3 navel oranges
1/3 cup bottled Italian dressing
2 large red onions

Add zest of one orange to dressing.

Peel oranges and onions and slice about one-quarter inch thick; place in a shallow dish or plastic bag and pour dressing over. Marinate, turning occasionally, for one or two hours.

Arrange orange and onion slices in an oiled grill basket and place on barbecue. Cook on High heat about three minutes per side. Drizzle any remaining dressing over the oranges and onions, just before serving.

Serve with pork, lamb or fish.

Patio Potatoes

4 servings

2 - 3 large potatoes
100 g (1/4 lb.) Cheddar cheese (optional)
1/2 large onion, thinly sliced
2 - 3 slices bacon, cooked and crumbled
Salt
Freshly ground black pepper
3 tbsp. butter or margarine

Scrub potatoes well; slice thinly. If using cheese, cut into half-inch cubes.

Grease a large sheet of heavy-duty foil. Spread half of potato slices on foil; top with onions, bacon and cheese. Season with salt and pepper. Cover with remaining potatoes and dot with butter.

Wrap foil package using the "drugstore wrap": Place food in the centre of a piece of foil large enough that when the ends are brought together, they can be folded in an interlocking seam. "Pleatfold" the long side and make an extra fold in the ends before pressing them against the package. Fold the foil to fit the food, but do not make it air-tight for barbecuing.

Barbecue potatoes about one hour on grill, turning several times, until potatoes are tender.

Foil-Wrapped Barbecued Veggies

8 servings

1 lb. carrots, cut into julienne strips
1 lb. green beans, cut into 2-inch pieces
1/2 lb. mushrooms, thickly sliced
1 small zucchini, sliced
1 tsp. seasoned salt
1/2 tsp. dried leaf thyme
2 tbsp. butter or margarine
2 tbsp. water

On a large sheet of heavy duty foil (or in a foil pan), combine carrots, beans, mushrooms and zucchini. Add seasonings, butter and water. Fold foil over vegetables, securely sealing the package, or tightly cover foil pan. Barbecue vegetables over medium-hot coals 50 minutes to one hour, turning package occasionally or stirring if using a foil pan.

Sweet Potatoes a l 'Orange

8 servings

2 lb. sweet potatoes (5-6) OR 2 cans (19 oz./540 mL each) sweet potatoes, drained
2 oranges
1 1/2 tsp. cornstarch
1/2 cup orange juice
2 tbsp. butter or margarine
2 tbsp. honey or brown sugar
1/8 tsp. cloves
Juice of 1 lime

Scrub, prick and microwave sweet potatoes on High power for 18-20 minutes or until tender. Let cool, peel and thickly slice into a two-litre microwavable casserole. Remove the zest (colored outer layer of rind) of one orange and set aside. Peel and slice oranges and arrange over sweet potatoes.

In a two-cup glass measure, combine cornstarch, orange juice, butter, honey and cloves. Cook on High 2 1/2 - 3 minutes, or until thickened and smooth. Stir every minute. Pour sauce over oranges; sprinkle with orange zest. Drizzle lime juice over top.

Cover with vented lid and cook on High seven to nine minutes or until heated through or bake at 300 - 350 degrees F for 20-30 minutes.

Turnip and Apple Casserole

The large plain-looking, globe-shaped vegetable with a waxed, dark outer skin and golden flesh is properly called rutabaga. Some of us will forever call it turnip.

8 servings

1 large rutabaga (about 1 kg)
1 tbsp. butter or margarine
2 apples
1/4 cup brown sugar
Pinch of cinnamon
1/3 cup flour
1/3 cup brown sugar
2 tbsp. butter

Peel, dice and cook rutabaga. Drain well and mash with one tablespoon butter. Peel and slice apples into thin wedges. Toss with one-quarter cup brown sugar and cinnamon.

Layer mashed rutabaga and apples in a two-litre buttered casserole, beginning and ending with rutabaga.

In a small bowl, combine flour and one-third cup sugar; cut two tablespoons butter into mixture; sprinkle over casserole. Bake at 350 degrees F for one hour.

Hot Herbed Tomatoes

6 servings

1/4 cup butter or margarine
1 tsp. brown sugar
1/2 tsp. salt
Dash freshly ground pepper
1/2 tsp. dried oregano
6 firm, ripe tomatoes, peeled and cored
1/3 cup finely chopped celery
2 - 3 tbsp. finely snipped parsley
2 tbsp. finely snipped fresh chives or 1 tsp. dried

Melt butter in a nine-inch skillet or large saucepan; add sugar, salt, pepper and oregano. Mix thoroughly.

Add tomatoes, cored side down; cover pan and simmer five minutes. Spoon butter mixture over tomatoes and add celery, parsley and chives. Cover and simmer 6 to 8 minutes longer.

Spoon sauce over tomatoes before serving.

Ratatouille Provencal

Ratatouille leftovers make an excellent filling for omelettes. Drain off the liquid that accumulates on standing.

6 - 8 servings

1/3 cup olive oil, divided
2 medium onions, sliced lengthwise
1 red and 1 green pepper, seeded and sliced
1 or 2 small eggplants, thinly sliced
2 cloves garlic, crushed
Salt and freshly ground pepper
4 - 5 small zucchini, sliced
4 - 6 medium tomatoes, sliced
1/4 tsp. each: savory and thyme
1/2 cup freshly grated Parmesan cheese

Place three tablespoons oil in a deep skillet and heat. Saute onions until lightly browned, add peppers, eggplant(s) and garlic. Season with salt and pepper and cook gently, stirring occasionally, until vegetables are softened.

Spread cooked vegetables in a two-litre baking dish. Top with a row of zucchini, then overlap with a row of tomatoes, repeating rows until dish is full. Sprinkle with savory and thyme and two tablespoons oil.

Bake uncovered for 30 minutes at 350 degrees F. Sprinkle with Parmesan and remaining oil; bake another 15 to 20 minutes.

Mandarin Rice

Cook the rice ahead of time for this attractive and easy side dish.

8 - 10 servings

1/4 cup margarine
1 - 2 stalks celery, sliced
2 cans (10 oz./284 mL each) mandarin oranges, well drained
4 - 5 cups cooked rice

Melt the margarine in a large skillet or saucepan.

Saute celery until tender-crisp. Add the drained oranges and rice.

Heat over medium-low heat, until rice is heated through (six to seven minutes if rice is hot, 10 minutes if rice is cold), stirring occasionally.

Sunny Carrot and Leek Casserole

This casserole of vegetables and rice is so attractive and cheery looking, it will brighten your day.

Leeks are not used as frequently as other members of the onion family. Their mild sweet flavor blends well with the other ingredients in this casserole. To prepare leeks, cut off root end and most of the green part — leave one to two inches of green. Rinse out all sand carefully and slice leeks about one-quarter inch thick.

Some of the ingredients in this recipe are precooked. Therefore, casserole could be cooked and assembled ahead of time, then reheated in the oven for 30 minutes.

7 - 8 servings

2 cups sliced carrots OR 1 can (14 oz./398 mL) small whole carrots
2 tbsp. butter or margarine
2 cups sliced leeks
3/4 cup uncooked converted, long grain rice
1 1/2 cups liquid*
1 tsp. chicken broth mix or liquid concentrate
Fresh parsley sprigs

*Drain liquid from canned or cooked carrots; add enough water to make one and one-half cups.

Place fresh carrots in a microwavable bowl; cover and cook on High power for five to six minutes, or until tender-crisp. Drain, reserving liquid.

Melt butter in a two-litre microwavable casserole on High (30 to 40 seconds). Add leeks, stirring to coat with butter; cover and microwave on High for three to four minutes; stirring once. Remove leeks with a slotted spoon and set aside.

Add rice, liquid and chicken broth mix to casserole; cover. Microwave on High for 10 to 12 minutes; let stand 10 minutes.

Stir in carrots and leeks. Cover and microwave on High three to four minutes. Let stand five minutes.

Or precook and assemble casserole early in the day, cover and refrigerate. Thirty to 40 minutes before serving, place casserole in conventional oven at 350 degrees F, or reheat in microwave at 70 to 80% (Medium-High) for six to seven minutes.

Herbed Rice Ring

So many of our favorite foods for entertaining can be prepared well ahead of serving. This lightly seasoned rice dish can too; prepare it early in the day or even a day or two before. Then reheat just before serving.

8 servings

2 tbsp. margarine or butter
1/4 cup finely chopped green onion
1 1/2 cups uncooked converted long grain rice
3 cups cold water
1/2 tsp. chicken bouillon powder or liquid concentrate
1/2 - 1 tsp. dried herb blend*
Dash freshly ground black pepper
2 tbsp. chopped pimento**

* Herb blend could be thyme with basil, parsley, oregano.

** Fresh, sweet chopped red pepper can be used in place of pimento when available. Use one-quarter cup and cook with onion, increasing the first cooking time to three minutes.

Combine margarine and onion in a deep two or three litre microwavable casserole. Cook on High power for 1 1/2 to 2 minutes, or until onion is tender; stir once. Stir in rice, water, chicken bouillon powder, herbs and pepper. Cover and cook on High for 13 to 15 minutes. (The rice will cook more quickly in a wide, shallow dish, but it may boil over; watch and if necessary, reduce power and increase cooking time.)

Let rice stand, covered, for 10 to 12 minutes. Check for doneness. If rice is tender, but still very moist, or if rice is not cooked, cook another two to three minutes. Let stand two to three minutes; all the water should be absorbed. Stir in pimento.

Press rice into a microwavable baking ring (1.5 litre) that has been well greased with margarine or butter. Cover and chill at least one hour.

Reheat rice, covered, on High for 5 1/2 to six minutes or until heated through. Let stand three to five minutes.

Run a knife around outer and inner edges of ring and invert rice onto a large serving plate. Fill centre with vegetable or main dish if desired.

DESSERTS

Apple Brown Betty With Honey

6 servings

6 large cooking apples (Spy, Cortland or Ida Red)
1/2 tsp. ground ginger
3/4 cup bran flakes
1/2 cup all purpose flour
1/2 cup brown sugar
1/4 cup butter
1/4 cup honey
2 tbsp. water
2 tsp. lemon juice

Peel, core and thinly slice apples. Place in a greased casserole; sprinkle with ginger.

In a separate bowl, stir cereal, flour and brown sugar together. Cut butter into mixture until crumbly. Distribute mixture evenly over apples. Combine honey, water and lemon juice in one-cup glass measure. Heat in microwave on High 30 to 45 seconds; pour over topping.

Bake at 350 degrees F for 45 minutes or until apples are tender. Serve warm, with ice cream if desired.

Poached Apples and Pears

5 - 6 servings

1/4 cup sugar
1/2 cup water
1 stick cinnamon
2 medium apples
2 medium pears

In a two-litre microwavable casserole, combine sugar, water and cinnamon stick. Let stand while preparing fruit.

Peel fruit if desired then cut into thin slices. Add fruit to sugar solution; cover dish and cook on High four to six minutes or until tender-crisp. Stir halfway through cooking.

Serve warm over pancakes or chill and serve with cookies or brownies.

Baked Apples Flambe

This is the most opulent version of baked apples we have ever tasted.

2 servings

1/4 cup corn syrup or honey
1/4 cup sugar
2 tbsp. marmalade
2 tbsp. butter or margarine
2 cooking apples
1/4 cup mincemeat
1 1/2 oz. brandy or rum

Combine corn syrup, sugar, marmalade and butter in a small saucepan and cook over medium heat, stirring constantly, until sugar is dissolved. Pour sauce into a small baking dish.

Wash and core apples; remove one strip of peel from top or around centre of apples. Place apples in syrup and fill centres with mincemeat.

Cover dish and bake at 375 degrees F for 25 minutes. Remove cover, baste with syrup. Bake uncovered, 10 to 15 minutes longer or until apples are tender. Keep warm until serving time.

Heat brandy in a small pan (even a metal ladle is big enough) until bubbles form. Ignite and pour flaming brandy over apples. If possible warm the brandy and flame it at the table as the flames don't last long. You can heat the brandy over a fondue burner or a candle warmer in a small container such as a butter warmer. And, of course, the flaming apples will be more spectacular if you are dining by candlelight.

Microwave Apple Crisp

5 servings

4 large apples, peeled and sliced
1 - 2 tbsp. sugar
2 tsp. lemon juice (optional)
1/2 cup all purpose flour
1/2 cup quick cooking oats
2/3 cup brown sugar
3/4 tsp. cinnamon
1/4 tsp. cloves
1/3 cup butter or margarine
1/4 cup chopped nuts (optional)

Put sliced apples in 1.5-litre microwavable casserole; sprinkle with sugar and lemon juice, if desired.

Combine flour, oats, brown sugar, cinnamon and cloves. Cut in butter until mixture is crumbly; add nuts if desired. Sprinkle crumb mixture over apples.

Cook on High power for 12 to 14 minutes, or until apples are tender and topping is browned and crisp. Let stand four to five minutes. Serve warm, with ice cream if desired.

Deep Dish Apple Crisp

For a quick and easy dessert try this apple crisp that is similar to a deep dish pie. Its secret is the corn syrup. It's delicious warm or cold, but warmed is best with a small amount of cream poured over top.

4 - 6 servings

4 - 6 large apples
1/4 cup corn syrup
1/4 cup water*
1/4 tsp. cinnamon or nutmeg (optional)
3/4 cup biscuit mix
1/2 cup brown sugar

*In late winter, when apples are soft, reduce water to one tablespoonful.

Peel, core and thinly slice apples into a greased two-litre casserole. Stir corn syrup and water together; drizzle over apples.

Combine biscuit mix and brown sugar; sprinkle over apples. Bake uncovered at 350 degrees F about 25 minutes. Serve warm with cream or ice cream.

Carrot Pudding

A Christmas tradition that can be made a month before the big day.

8 - 10 servings

1 cup raisins
1 cup currants
$1^1/_2$ cups all purpose flour
1 cup brown sugar
1 tsp. baking soda
1 tsp. salt
1 large carrot, grated
1 large potato, grated
1 large apple, peeled and grated or finely chopped
1 cup suet
$^1/_4$ cup chopped nuts (optional)
$^3/_4$ cup cut mixed fruit or peel (optional)
2 - 4 tbsp. brandy (optional)

Thoroughly grease a two-litre casserole or pudding mould (or two one-litre moulds).

Rinse the raisins and currants; drain well and pat dry. Set aside.

Combine flour, sugar, baking soda and salt in a large mixing bowl. Stir in the carrot, potato and apple as soon as they are grated (the potato and apple will discolor quickly).

Add suet, raisins, currants, nuts, peel and brandy, if desired; mix well.

Put pudding mixture in prepared dishes, cover with a lid or tie a piece of heavy foil (greased on the underside) securely over dish.

Steam over or in simmering water for four hours. Remove cover and let pudding cool completely.

Cover pudding securely and store in a cold place until a few hours before you want to serve it.

Reheat pudding over or in simmering water for $1^1/_2$ hours. Unmould and serve with a pudding sauce such as the following.

BROWN SUGAR SAUCE

Makes $1^2/_3$ cups

1 cup brown sugar
2 tbsp. cornstarch
Dash salt
$^1/_2$ tsp. nutmeg
$1^1/_2$ cups hot water
1 tbsp. lemon juice
2 tbsp. butter
1 tsp. vanilla or rum extract OR 1 - 2 tbsp. brandy or rum

Combine sugar, cornstarch, salt and nutmeg in a four-cup glass measure or 1.5-litre microwavable bowl. Stir in water and cook on High power for three to four minutes, or until sauce is thickened and clear; stir two or three times during cooking.

Add lemon juice, butter and flavoring or brandy. Serve warm over carrot pudding.

Mincemeat Flambe

Glamorous, but easy.

6 - 8 servings

2 cups prepared mincemeat
1/4 cup orange juice
1/4 cup marachino cherries, drained and chopped
1/3 cup nuts (pecans or almonds)
1/4 cup brandy or cognac
Vanilla ice cream

Combine mincemeat, orange juice, cherries and nuts in a clear glass one-litre microwavable bowl. Cook on High power for three to four minutes, or until mixture is bubbly.

Warm brandy in a one cup glass measure on High power for about 15 seconds, or just until bubbles begin to form around edge. Dim the lights; ignite brandy and pour over hot mincemeat mixture.

Serve over ice cream while sauce is still flaming.

> Do not use a crystal bowl in the microwave. The bowl will shatter due to its lead content.

Fruit-Filled Puffy Pancake

This is a most interesting dish to watch while it cooks — as the batter cooks, it pushes up the sides and ends of the pan to to make the basket that holds the fruit.

6 - 8 servings

2 tbsp. margarine or butter
5 eggs
1 cup all purpose flour
1 cup milk
1/2 tsp. salt
4 - 5 large apples (delicious or spy)
1 can (19oz./540 mL) sliced peaches, drained
3 tbsp. brown sugar
1/2 tsp. cinnamon
1/2 tsp. nutmeg
1 cup shredded Swiss cheese

Put margarine in baking pan (13 x 9 inches or 12 x 9 inches) and place in oven at 425 degrees F (400 degrees F for glass pan) until melted. Remove pan from oven and tilt to coat with margarine.

Combine eggs, flour, milk and salt in blender and mix until smooth. Scrape down sides of blender to be sure all flour is incorporated. Pour batter into pan and bake (in lower third of oven, but not at the bottom) for 20 minutes.

Meanwhile peel, core and cut apples into eighths. Place in covered two-litre microwavable dish and cook on High five to six minutes or until apples are tender but not soft.

Stir in peaches, brown sugar, cinnamon and nutmeg, cover. Reheat on 70 per cent power (Medium High) about one or two minutes just prior to pouring fruit mixture into pancake "basket."

Sprinkle with cheese and place in oven until cheese melts. Serve immediately.

Warm Blueberry Grunt

When steamed on top of the stove, these dumplings "grunt" and hence the unglamorous name of this dessert. We updated this old Maritime recipe for the microwave oven; the fan motor noise is louder than any sound the dumplings make, but they do give a little groan when the dish is removed from the oven.

Cook this dessert just before eating your main course so it will be warm.

6 - 8 servings

1/2 cup sugar
1 tsp. cornstarch
2 1/2 - 4 cups blueberries
1 tsp. lemon juice

Dumplings:

2 cups all purpose flour
3 tsp. baking powder
1/4 tsp. salt
1/2 tsp. nutmeg
1/4 cup shortening
1 egg
2/3 cup milk

In a deep, two-litre microwavable casserole, stir together sugar and cornstarch.

Wash and pick over blueberries; stir into sugar mixture. Add lemon juice. Cook, uncovered, on High power for 3 1/2 to five minutes or just until mixture boils; stir once during cooking.

Meanwhile, stir together flour, baking powder, salt and nutmeg. Cut in shortening until mixture is crumbly. Beat together egg and milk and stir into dry ingredients to make a soft dough (add a little more milk if necessary).

Drop six to eight dumplings by tablespoonfuls over hot blueberry sauce. Cover casserole with a high, domed lid (such as another, inverted casserole); do not vent. Cook at 70-per-cent power (Medium-High) for six minutes, or until dumplings are puffed and dry on top.

Serve warm with cream or whipped cream. If not serving immediately, let stand, loosely covered.

Happy Endings, Barbecue Style

There is no reason to limit outdoor cooking to meat and vegetables. Dessert can be prepared on the barbecue too, and if you serve a flaming dessert, just after dark, your guests will be impressed by your showmanship as well as your culinary ability.

HOT FRUIT SHORTCAKE

4 - 6 servings

1/4 cup butter or margarine
3 green-tipped bananas, peeled and quartered OR 3 - 4 firm peaches or nectarines, cut in wedges
2 tbsp. lemon juice
1/2 cup brown sugar
1/4 tsp. cinnamon
4 - 6 slices poundcake, 3/4 inch thick
1/4 cup fruit-flavored liqueur, brandy or light rum (optional)
Ice cream or sour cream (optional)

Melt butter in pan on hot barbecue. Add prepared fruit, drizzle with lemon juice and sprinkle with sugar and cinnamon. Cook until fruit is slightly softened, spoon syrup over fruit occasionally.

Meanwhile, toast poundcake (both sides) on the grill.

To flame, warm the liqueur in a small pan until bubbles form; ignite. Pour flaming liqueur over fruit.

To serve, place toasted poundcake slices on plates, spoon fruit and syrup over. Top with ice cream or a dollop of sour cream if desired.

WAIKIKI PINEAPPLE

6 - 8 servings

1 fresh pineapple
15 - 20 whole cloves
1/2 cup maple syrup
1/2 tsp. cinnamon
1/4 cup fruit flavored liqueur, brandy or rum (optional)

Remove skin and "eyes" from pineapple, but leave leafy crown intact, except for a few spikes right in the centre. Wrap the crown in foil to prevent scorching. Stud the surface of the pineapple with cloves. Insert rotisserie spit through centre of pineapple, lengthwise (this is the most difficult step as the core is very hard); secure with holding forks.

Combine syrup and cinnamon; set aside.

Barbecue pineapple over low heat for about one hour, basting often with the syrup. When pineapple is heated through, remove it from the spit, unwrap crown and dip it in water to cool for easier handling. Slice pineapple into circles or wedges.

To flame, warm liqueur in a small pan; ignite and pour over pineapple. Serve warm.

Spiced Plum Compote

Fruit compotes are an excellent dessert choice for early autumn. Apples, pears and peaches are also suitable for poaching.

4 - 5 servings

18 prune plums ($1^1/_4$ to $1^1/_2$ pounds)
$^1/_3$ cup anise or vanilla sugar*
$^3/_4$ cup water
1 cinnamon stick, broken
4 thin strips of orange peel
$^1/_4$ cup dried currants
1 tbsp. apricot brandy
Cream (optional)

*To make anise sugar, crush one teaspoon anise seeds and stir into one-third cup sugar. Or you could use plain sugar and add a vanilla bean to the syrup.

Wash plums; cut into halves and remove pits. Combine plums, sugar, water, cinnamon stick, orange peel and currants in a medium saucepan. Heat to boiling, stirring occasionally to dissolve sugar. Reduce heat and simmer gently for 10 to 12 minutes, or until plums are just tender.

Using a slotted spoon, remove plums to a serving bowl.

Boil syrup for eight to 10 minutes, or until slightly thickened. Remove cinnamon stick and orange rind (and vanilla bean if used). Stir brandy into syrup and pour syrup over plums.

Serve compote warm or chilled; drizzle with cream if desired.

Chocolate Fondue

Fresh fruit such as bananas, strawberries, kiwi, pears and pineapple are exquisite dipped in melted chocolate. If there is some chocolate left over, cover and refrigerate it; warm it in microwave or in a double boiler for a quick dessert.

4 to 6 servings

1/3 cup light cream (10% M.F.)
300 g Toberlone or sweet chocolate bar or cooking chocolate
Dash cinnamon
1 or 2 tbsp. brandy
Fresh fruit

Heat cream and chocolate in microwave on 50% (Medium-Low) power until chocolate just begins to melt. Stir to finish melting chocolate. Stir in cinnamon and brandy.

Pour mixture into pottery fondue pot and place over fondue heater on very low flame. Serve with a platter of fresh fruit or cubes of pound cake or tiny macaroons.

Hot Judge Pudding

6 servings

1 cup all Eleanor's Basic Biscuit Mix (see page 213)
1/2 cup sugar
1/2 cup cocoa, divided
1/2 cup milk
1 tsp. vanilla
1/2 cup brown sugar
1 1/3 cups hot water
Icing sugar (optional)

In a two-litre microwavable cake pan, mix together: biscuit mix, sugar and one-quarter cup cocoa. Add milk and vanilla and stir until well blended. Combine remaining one-quarter cup cocoa and brown sugar and sprinkle evenly over batter. Pour water over topping.

Cook at 50 per cent (Medium-Low) power for eight minutes, rotating pan once or twice during cooking if necessary. Increase power to High and cook another three to four minutes, or until almost dry on top. Let stand 10 minutes.

Dust with icing sugar if desired. Serve pudding warm, with whipped cream or ice cream if desired.

Lemon Sponge Pudding

Perhaps everyone's Mom made a version of this old-fashioned dessert. The method given here is not the standard one found in most cook-books, but comes as close as I can get to my Mom's. For Pat, this dessert epitomizes comfort food; it has been her favorite dessert since childhood.

As it cooks, this light, delectable pudding separates into a sponge layer on top with lots of tangy lemon sauce underneath.

4 servings

1 1/2 tbsp. butter or margarine
3/4 - 1 cup sugar*
2 tbsp. all purpose flour
Grated rind and juice of 1 lemon
1 - 1 1/4 cups milk*
2 eggs separated

*Use the greater or lesser amount of sugar according to your sweet tooth. Mother's recipe listed one cup of milk with directions to "add more"!

Cream butter and mix in sugar as thoroughly as possible. Stir in flour, lemon rind, juice and milk. Add beaten egg yolks and mix well.

Beat egg whites until soft peaks form; fold into custard mixture. Pour into a 1.5-litre casserole.

Set casserole inside a larger pan of water; the water should come up to the level of the pudding.

Oven-poach at 375 degrees F about 40 minutes or until a knife inserted near the centre comes out clean.

Serve warm or chilled.

Gwen's Lime Cheesecake

Quark is a natural, skim milk, white cheese. It is similar to cream cheese, but has a crumbly texture and is lower in calories. It can be substituted for cream cheese in many recipes.

10 - 12 servings

Crust:

1 1/2 cups shredded coconut
2 tbsp. butter or margarine, at room temperature

Filling:

1 envelope unflavored gelatin
3/4 cup frozen limeade concentrate, thawed (but not diluted)
1/2 - 3/4 cup sugar
250 g Quark cheese
Green food coloring
500 mL whipping cream, divided
2 egg whites, stiffly beaten (optional)

Garnish:

Fresh lime, thinly sliced
Chocolate-Dipped Strawberries (see page 161)

Crust: Combine coconut and butter. Pat evenly into bottom of a round, nine-inch springform pan. Bake at 350 degree F for eight to 10 minutes, or until golden brown. Cool.

Filling: In a small saucepan, sprinkle gelatin over limeade concentrate. Let stand two to three minutes. Add one-half cup sugar and heat until sugar and gelatin are dissolved.

Beat cheese until light and fluffy; stir in gelatin mixture. Add two to three drops of food coloring to obtain a pale green color. Taste and add more sugar if desired; beat well. Chill until partially set.

Beat one cup whipping cream until stiff. Fold into gelatin mixture. Fold in stiffly beaten egg whites if desired. (The egg whites will make a slightly lighter cheesecake, but they are not essential.) Pour filling over cooled crust. Chill until firm.

Garnish: Remove cheesecake from pan to a serving plate. Whip remaining cream until stiff. Spread over cheesecake and garnish with Chocolate Dipped Strawberries and lime "twists." (Make one slit into centre of each lime slice and twist open ends in opposite directions).

Chocolate Dipped Strawberries

People accustomed to working with chocolate know that moisture and chocolate don't mix: the chocolate becomes thicker, not thinner, and dull. Therefore, the berries in this recipe must be washed several hours before dipping, and spread on paper towels to dry thoroughly. If the berries are not dirty or sandy,brush them gently with a soft brush and use as little water as possible.

To prevent moisture from getting into the chocolate as it melts, use a microwave oven rather than a double boiler. If you must use a double boiler, have the water barely simmering, not boiling, and do not let the top pan touch the water.

To avoid over-cooking or scorching the chocolate, use 50 per cent power (Medium or Medium-Low) and leave the chocolate uncovered to prevent condensation.

Makes about 25

1 1/2 pints fresh strawberries, with hulls and stems if possible
1 cup semi-sweet chocolate chips
1 tsp. butter

Clean berries as directed above.Cover a cookie sheet or tray with waxed paper.

Place chocolate chips in a dry, shallow dish or bowl, with butter in centre. Heat at 50 per cent power (Medium-Low), uncovered, until most of the chocolate turns from dull to shiny. Remove from microwave, stir, and if all chips are not melted, heat another 30 to 60 seconds.

Hold berries by the stem (if necessary, insert a skewer into berry through the hull), and dip each one into the melted chocolate, so that at least half of the berry is coated. Allow excess chocolate to drip off, and place the coated berry on its side on the waxed paper. If the chocolate becomes too firm while you work, warm it for a few seconds.

Refrigerate dipped berries for 30 minutes to harden the chocolate. Remove, and if necessary, store a few hours in a cool place. If left in the refrigerator too long, chocolate becomes dull.

Apple Cheesecake Viennoise

The cheesecake base is a rich pastry. It is advisable to brush the partly cooked pastry with some stirred egg white to prevent the filling from soaking into the pastry.

10 - 12 servings

Crust:

- **1 cup flour**
- **1/4 cup sugar**
- **1 tsp. grated lemon rind**
- **1/2 cup butter**
- **1 egg, separated**
- **1/4 tsp. vanilla**

Filling:

- **2 packages (250 g each) cream cheese**
- **1/2 cup sugar**
- **2 eggs**
- **1/2 tsp. vanilla**

Topping:

- **4 cups thick applesauce***
- **1/3 cup sugar**
- **1/2 tsp. cinnamon**
- **1/4 tsp. nutmeg**
- **1/2 cup sliced almonds**
- **250 mL whipping cream, whipped (optional)**

* Applesauce must be thick and may be chunky if desired.

Crust: Combine flour, sugar and rind in food processor or large mixing bowl. Add butter to processor or cut in with pastry blender until mixture is crumbly. Add egg yolk and vanilla and blend thoroughly.

Pat one-third of dough on bottom of nine- or 10-inch spring form pan, side removed. Bake at 400 degrees F for eight minutes or until golden. Cool. Brush lightly with stirred egg white. Attach ring to bottom of pan, butter side lightly and pat remaining dough about one inch up sides.

Filling: Combine cream cheese, sugar, eggs and vanilla in food processor or mixing bowl. Process or beat until creamy and well blended. Pour into spring-form pan.

Topping: Stir applesauce, sugar, cinnamon and nutmeg together. Spread over cream cheese layer. Top with sliced almonds.

Bake at 400 degrees F for 10 minutes; reduce heat to 350 degrees F and bake 25-35 minutes longer, or until centre has set. Cool. Top each serving with a dollop of whipped cream if desired.

Strawberries Romanoff

A premier dessert!

6 - 8 servings

$1^1/_2$ quarts strawberries, washed and hulled
Super fine sugar (fruit sugar) to taste
$^1/_2$ cup whipping cream
1 cup vanilla ice cream, slightly softened*
2 tbsp. orange-flavored liqueur
1 tbsp. lemon juice

*Be sure to use good quality ice cream.

Place strawberries in a glass serving dish and sprinkle lightly with sugar. Cover and chill one hour.

About 10 minutes before serving, whip cream until stiff. Fold in ice cream, liqueur and lemon juice until well blended, but still foamy. Pour sauce over strawberries, or serve separately in a chilled bowl.

Fruit Salad With Yogurt Topping

Virtually all fruits are compatible; you can decide while shopping which ones to use in this and similar recipes, depending on availability, quality and price on any given day. Sweetened yogurt is an easy and nutritious fruit topping.

4 - 5 servings

Zest of 1 orange
2 tbsp. honey
1 cup plain yogurt
1 - 2 oranges
1 cup cubed cantaloupe
1 - 2 bananas, sliced

Stir orange zest and honey into yogurt; let stand 15 minutes at room temperature or longer in the refrigerator, to blend flavors.

Peel orange(s), removing white pith; section or slice (remove seeds if necessary). Combine orange(s), melon and banana(s) in serving bowl. Top with yogurt mixture.

Fruit for a Crowd

Makes about 14 cups

- **$^1/_2$ cup orange juice**
- **$^1/_2$ cup pineapple juice**
- **Juice of $^1/_2$ lemon**
- **$^1/_4$ - $^1/_3$ cup apricot brandy**
- **1 can (10 oz./284 mL) mandarin oranges, drained**
- **2 cups (1 pint) blueberries, washed**
- **2 - 3 kiwi fruit**
- **1 mango**
- **2 cups (1 pint) strawberries**
- **1 large canteloupe**
- **1 large honey dew melon**
- **$^1/_4$ watermelon**
- **6 peaches**
- **2 nectarines (optional)**
- **3 bananas (optional)**

In a very large (five- to six-litre) bowl or container, combine juices and brandy. Add mandarins and blueberries.

Peel kiwis, cut in half lengthwise and slice crosswise. Peel mango and cut into half-inch cubes. Clean and hull strawberries and cut in half. Remove seeds from melons and cut into balls or cubes. Peel peaches and slice. Slice nectarines and bananas, if used.

As each fruit is prepared, add it to the juices to prevent discoloration; stir mixture gently to blend.

Cover container and chill until ready to serve. Serve in a hollowed out watermelon, or a clear glass bowl.

Minted Oranges and Grapes

6 - 8 servings

- **$^1/_2$ cup liquid honey**
- **Juice of 1 large lemon**
- **2 tbsp. snipped fresh mint**
- **3 navel oranges, peeled**
- **2 cups (about $^3/_4$ lb. or 350 g) seedless green grapes**
- **Mint sprigs for garnish**

Combine honey, lemon juice and mint in medium bowl.

Slice oranges and cut into half or quarter slices, depending on size. Stir orange slices and grapes into honey mixture. Cover and chill two hours or longer. Garnish with fresh mint sprigs.

Melon Ball Compote

Lemon juice enhances, but does not change, the flavor of the melon balls. The sugar counteracts the tartness of the lemon and makes the melon balls shine.

8 servings

1 canteloupe
1 honeydew melon
1/4 watermelon
Juice of 1 lemon
1 - 1 1/2 tbsp. super-fine sugar (fruit sugar)
Orange flavored liqueur (optional)
Fresh mint leaves

Remove seeds from canteloupe and honeydew melons. Press a melon ball cutter into the melons and rotate the head to form a perfectly round ball. Work around and between the seeds in the watermelon.

Drizzle lemon juice over melon and sprinkle with sugar; if desired, drizzle with liqueur. Stir gently.

Cover and chill at least one hour. Garnish with mint leaves.

Jo's Fruit Dip

Summer meals at the Nunans' are invariably eaten outdoors where we can enjoy John's beautiful garden. Fresh berries or other fruits with dip are often served — either as an appetizer or as dessert.

Makes 1 cup

1 cup sour cream
1/2 cup icing sugar
1 tsp. lemon juice
1/2 - 1 tsp. grated lemon rind
Fresh strawberries, washed but not hulled

Mix together sour cream, sugar, lemon juice and rind; put into a pretty serving dish and set it in the centre of a tray of berries. Jo's directions: "Dip to your stomach's delight."

Orange Fruit Dip

This rich, custardy fruit dip is cooked. It is delicious with strawberries, sliced peaches, nectarines, apples, bananas or spears of pineapple. It can be cooked in a double boiler over simmering water, as well as by microwave.

Makes 2 cups

1/3 cup butter or margarine
1/4 cup sugar
Grated rind of 2 oranges
1/2 cup fresh orange juice
1 tbsp. lemon juice
4 eggs

In a six- or eight-cup microwavable bowl, melt butter on High power for 50 to 60 seconds. In a deep bowl, beat together sugar, orange rind and juice, lemon juice and eggs; stirring constantly, pour this mixture into hot butter.

Cook sauce at 50 per cent power (Medium or Medium-Low) for 3 1/2 to 4 1/2 minutes. Stir after 1 1/2 minutes, then every 30 seconds until mixture begins to thicken. Do not let it boil or it will curdle.

Let dip stand, covered, for 10 minutes; stir. Dip should be the consistency of a soft pudding. Cover and chill.

Place a bowl of dip in the centre of a tray of prepared fruits. (Dip apples, peaches, nectarines, and bananas in fruit juice to prevent discoloration.)

Baked Orange Flans

In Europe, a flan is a custard or cream pudding. Creme caramel is a classic recipe, excellent for entertaining. The dessert must be cooled at least three hours, and preferably overnight, before serving.

4 - 5 servings

Caramel:

1/2 cup sugar
2 tsp. hot water

Custard:

2 cups milk
3 eggs
1/2 cup sugar
1 tsp. orange-flavored liqueur
Dash salt
Zest of one orange

Caramel: Place sugar in a small, heavy saucepan and cook over medium heat until sugar melts and turns a light golden brown. Remove from heat; add water carefully down the side of the pan; stir well. Pour the hot caramel into dry ramekins, swirl each to coat the bottom and part of the sides with caramel. Set aside.

Custard: Place milk in top of a double boiler and heat until bubbles form around edge of pot, or heat in microwave to 185 degrees F, using temperature probe or microwavable thermometer.

Beat eggs until frothy, add sugar, liqueur and salt; mix well. Gradually add hot milk to eggs, stirring constantly. Pour egg mixture evenly into ramekin cups.

Set ramekins in 13 x 9 inch baking dish; add hot water to reach halfway up the sides of the cups. Bake at 350 degrees F for 35 to 45 minutes or until knife inserted in centre of custard comes out clean.

Remove ramekins from water; cool then chill at least three hours or overnight.

To serve: Loosen edges of custards with a sharp knife and invert onto individual dessert plates. Garnish each flan with orange zest.

Pumpkin-Pecan Flan

Special holidays call for special food and this is a sensational dessert when topped with velvety rich custard sauce! Try it for Thanksgiving dinner.

10 servings

2 cups brown sugar, divided
3 tbsp. butter
1/4 cup water
1 can (28 oz./796 mL) pumpkin OR 3 1/2 cups cooked, mashed pumpkin
3/4 tsp. salt
1 tsp. ground cloves
3 tsp. cinnamon
1 1/2 tsp. ginger
1/2 tsp. allspice
Grated rind of 1 lemon
5 eggs, well beaten
2 3/4 cups evaporated milk
1 1/4 cups chopped pecans
Pecan halves for garnish

Preheat oven to 325 degrees F. Select a pan large and deep enough to hold a three-litre bowl and fill pan with hot water so water comes to about one inch from top of bowl.

Combine three-quarter cup of the brown sugar and butter in saucepan; cook over medium heat, stirring constantly, until mixture boils. Boil one minute, stirring; then slowly and very carefully, add water and boil mixture four minutes.

Warm a three-litre round mould (or mixing bowl) in the pan of hot water and pour in the sugar mixture. Immediately tilt bowl in all directions to coat bottom and sides with caramel. Remove bowl from water and set aside.

Mix pumpkin and remaining sugar, salt, spices and lemon rind. Add beaten eggs, evaporated milk and chopped pecans; stir until well mixed. Pour pumpkin mixture into caramelized bowl and place in pan of hot water in oven.

Bake two hours or until centre is firm. Cool, then chill overnight. To unmould, set the dish in a pan of warm water and loosen with a spatula or table knife. Invert onto platter and decorate top and around bottom edge with pecan halves. Serve with Rich Custard Sauce.

RICH CUSTARD SAUCE

Makes 2 cups

500 mL whipping cream
1 vanilla bean or 1 1/2 tsp. vanilla extract
1/3 cup sugar
3 egg yolks
1/4 tsp. salt

Heat cream to simmering. If using vanilla bean, split it lengthwise and simmer in cream for five minutes.

Combine sugar, egg yolks and salt; blend in a little hot cream, then stir this mixture into hot cream. Add vanilla extract if used. Cook custard in double boiler, over simmering water, until sauce is thick enough to coat a spoon. Remove vanilla bean.

Serve sauce warm or cold in a pretty pitcher, stand back and graciously accept the oohs and ahhs!

Peach Melba

It is difficult to have peaches at the exact degree of ripeness for this simple dessert. Poaching the peaches guarantees tender, tasty fruit.

5 - 6 servings

2 cups (1 pint) fresh OR 300 g frozen raspberries
2 tbsp. super-fine sugar
1 - 2 tbsp. brandy, to taste
1/2 cup water
1/2 cup sugar
1/2 tsp. vanilla
2 - 3 fresh peaches
Vanilla ice cream

Press raspberries through a sieve to remove seeds. Stir in super-fine sugar and brandy; set aside to allow flavors to blend.

Use a large diameter saucepan to hold peach halves in a single layer; add water, sugar and vanilla. Heat to boiling.

Peel peaches, cut in half and remove pits; add to hot syrup and poach five to six minutes, or until tender. Remove from heat; let stand in syrup until needed.

The dessert may be assembled with warm or chilled peaches. Put one or two scoops ice cream in each dessert dish; place a peach half, rounded side up, over ice cream. Spoon raspberry sauce over top and serve immediately.

Layered Sundae Squares

Like many favorite "company" dessert recipes, this is prepared ahead of time and comes out of the freezer just a few minutes before serving. It is simple to make, cuts and serves easily and is delicious.

Vanilla ice cream is always popular, but you could use any favorite flavor, or even different flavors, in the two ice cream layers; just be sure to buy the ice cream in rectangular "bricks".

12 servings

1 can (385 mL) 2% evaporated milk
1 package (250 g) miniature marshmallows
1 cup semisweet chocolate chips
1 cup flaked coconut*
2 cups graham wafer crumbs
½ cup margarine or butter, melted
2 L ice cream
1 cup chopped pecans

*Flaked coconut is in smaller, softer pieces than shredded, and larger than desiccated. If you can't find it, chop some shredded coconut. It can be lightly toasted (in the oven) if desired.

In an eight-cup glass measure (or in top of a double boiler) combine evaporated milk, marshmallows and chocolate chips. Heat five to six minutes at 60 to 70 per cent (Medium-High) power, stirring three or four times (or cook over simmering water) until marshmallows are melted.

Cool sauce to room temperature (it must be pourable, but not hot enough to melt the ice cream).

In medium bowl, combine coconut, crumbs and melted margarine. Set aside one cup of this mixture; press remainder onto bottom of a 13 by nine inch glass dish or baking pan.

Cut ice cream into one-half inch thick slices; arrange a single layer of ice cream slices over crumb crust. Pour about two cups of chocolate sauce over ice cream. Repeat ice cream and sauce layers.

Add pecans to reserved crumbs; sprinkle over dessert, pressing topping into sauce gently with flat edge of a spatula.

Cover pan with foil wrap; freeze until firm. Let dessert stand at room temperature five to eight minutes before slicing.

Merry-Go-Round Sundaes

For an easy summer dessert, make-your-own sundaes are hard to beat. We arrange a selection of toppings, including nuts, fruit and sauces on a lazy Susan and call them Merry-Go-Round Sundaes.

These sauces are two of our all-time favorites.

WONDERFUL FUDGE SAUCE

Makes about 3 cups

3 squares unsweetened chocolate
$1\frac{1}{2}$ cups sugar
$\frac{1}{4}$ tsp. salt
Pinch cream of tartar
$1\frac{1}{3}$ cups evaporated milk
$\frac{1}{2}$ cup butter or margarine
1 tsp. vanilla

Melt chocolate in top of double boiler. Add sugar, salt, cream of tartar and milk; stir. Let simmer five minutes.

Remove from heat; beat in butter and vanilla. Serve over ice cream, eclairs or plain cake. Refrigerate remaining sauce.

BUTTERSCOTCH SAUCE

Makes $2\frac{1}{2}$ cups

$1\frac{1}{2}$ cups brown sugar
$\frac{1}{2}$ cup light corn syrup
$\frac{1}{3}$ cup butter
$\frac{1}{2}$ teaspoon vanilla
$\frac{2}{3}$ cup evaporated milk

Combine brown sugar, corn syrup, butter and vanilla in a saucepan.

Cook mixture three to four minutes or until it reaches the soft ball stage (115 degrees C or 235-240 degrees F on a candy thermometer).

Cool five minutes; blend in evaporated milk.

Serve over ice cream. Refrigerate remaining sauce.

Chocolate Chip Zucchini Cupcakes

You can use a food processor to grate the zucchini and to mix the remaining ingredients together. An electric mixer or hand mixer works equally well. These cupcakes are great for lunch carriers as they don't require icing.

Makes 18 cupcakes

2 cups grated zucchini*
3 eggs
2 cups brown sugar
1 cup vegetable oil
1 tbsp. vanilla
2 cups all purpose flour
2 tsp. cinnamon
2 tsp. baking soda
1/4 teaspoon baking powder
1 tsp. salt
3/4 cup chopped nuts (optional)
1 cup semi-sweet chocolate chips

*Remove skin from zucchini if it is mature and thick.

If using a food processor, grate zucchini, measure and set aside.

Put eggs, sugar, oil and vanilla in food processor; using steel blade, process two to three seconds.

In a separate bowl, stir together flour, cinnamon, baking soda, baking powder and salt. Add to food processor and process just to mix, two to three seconds. Add zucchini, nuts and chocolate chips; process another two to three seconds or just until mixed.

Spoon batter into lightly greased muffin cups, filling at least three-quarters full. Bake at 350 degrees F for 15 to 20 minutes or until done. Store in a covered container.

Chocolate Sauerkraut Judge Cake

This cake has an unusual ingredient — sauerkraut — yet there is no trace (taste or smell) of the sauerkraut. Try it, you'll like it!

Makes 12-cup bundt pan

1 cup sauerkraut
1 1/4 cups butter or margarine
2 1/4 cups sugar
6 eggs
1 1/2 tsp. vanilla
4 1/2 cups sifted cake and pastry flour
3/4 tsp. baking soda
3/4 tsp. baking powder
1 tsp. salt
1 cup cocoa
2 cups water

Rinse and drain sauerkraut. Squeeze out liquid by hand, separate strands and chop. Cream butter in a large mixing bowl, add sugar and beat well. Add eggs, one at a time, beating after each; add vanilla and mix.

In a separate bowl, stir together flour, baking soda, baking powder, salt and cocoa. Add dry ingredients to creamed mixture alternately with water; stir in sauerkraut by hand if you have been using an electric mixer. Pour batter into an oiled 12-cup bundt pan.

Bake at 375 degrees F for 45 to 50 minutes or until cake tests done. Let stand 10 to 15 minutes, then loosen edges with a knife and invert cake onto a cooling rack. Ice with chocolate butter icing and serve with ice cream.

This cake freezes well but do not ice until cake is thawed.

Note: Some bundt pans stick unless greased properly. Pour about one tablespoon of vegetable oil into pan, then using a paper towel spread the oil in and around the pan's nooks and crannies.

Harvest Spice Cake

No icing required!

Makes 10-inch tube cake

1 cup butter or margarine, at room temperature
1 cup sugar
Grated rind of 1 orange
3 eggs
2½ cups cake and pastry flour
1 tsp. baking soda
1 tsp. baking powder
½ tsp. salt
1 tsp. cinnamon
¼ tsp. allspice
1 cup raisins
1 cup chopped nuts
1 cup sour cream
1 medium cooking apple, finely chopped

In large mixer bowl, cream butter, sugar and orange rind until fluffy. Add eggs, one at a time, beating well after each. Continue beating until mixture is very light. Sift the flour before measuring, then combine flour with baking soda, baking powder, salt, cinnamon and allspice.

Toss raisins and nuts with approximately one-half cup of the dry ingredients. Stir together the sour cream and apple.

Add the dry ingredients to creamed mixture alternately with the sour cream-apple mixture. Use approximately one-third of the quantity each time, beginning and ending with flour.

Stir in raisins and nuts, mixing just until all the flour is blended in. Pour the batter into a greased 10-inch tube pan. Bake at 350 degrees F for 55 to 60 minutes or until cake tests done.

Cool cake 10 minutes in pan. Turn out onto a cake rack to cool completely. Dust the top with icing sugar, if desired, just before serving.

Rhubarb Puddle Cake

Rhubarb and chives are the first signs of a new growing season in our garden. From early May to mid July, rhubarb appears on our tables frequently, in many types of desserts.

"Puddle" cake is a descriptive name for this recipe as the topping sinks into the batter, forming small depressions as it bakes. The cake travels well, so is good picnic or cottage fare.

Makes 7½ by 11½ inch pan or 9-inch square pan

Topping:

- **3 tbsp. butter or margarine**
- **1½ tsp. cinnamon**
- **¾ cup brown sugar**

Batter:

- **½ cup margarine**
- **1⅓ cups sugar**
- **1 egg**
- **1 tsp. vanilla**
- **2 cups all purpose flour**
- **1 tsp. baking soda**
- **¼ tsp. salt**
- **1 cup buttermilk**
- **2 cups chopped rhubarb**
- **1 tbsp. flour**

Topping: Blend butter, cinnamon and brown sugar together and set aside.

Batter: Cream margarine and sugar together. Beat in egg and vanilla.

Stir two cups flour, baking soda and salt together; add to creamed mixture alternately with buttermilk, beginning and ending with flour.

Toss rhubarb with one tablespoon flour and fold into batter. Spread batter in a greased baking pan.

Sprinkle topping over batter. Bake at 350 degrees F for 45 minutes, or until cake tests done. Let cool in pan set on wire rack.

Pumpkin Cake

Youngsters will be delighted with a cake that looks like a jack-o-lantern.

12 - 16 servings

Cake:

- **6 eggs, separated**
- **$^{1}/_{4}$ tsp. cream of tartar**
- **1$^{1}/_{2}$ cups sugar, divided**
- **2 cups sifted cake and pastry flour**
- **1 tbsp. baking powder**
- **1 tsp. salt**
- **$^{1}/_{2}$ tsp. each of nutmeg, ginger, cloves, allspice and cinnamon**
- **$^{1}/_{2}$ cup canned pumpkin**
- **$^{1}/_{2}$ cup vegetable oil**
- **$^{1}/_{2}$ cup water**

Frosting:

- **2 egg whites**
- **$^{3}/_{4}$ cup sugar**
- **$^{1}/_{3}$ cup corn syrup**
- **2 tbsp. water**
- **$^{1}/_{4}$ tsp. cream of tartar**
- **$^{1}/_{4}$ tsp. salt**
- **Yellow, red and green food coloring**
- **1 cup icing sugar**
- **$^{1}/_{4}$ cup cocoa**
- **1 small banana**

Cake: Beat egg whites with cream of tartar until soft peaks form. Add a half cup sugar, one tablespoon at a time, beating and mixing thoroughly after each addition. Whites should stand in firm peaks. Set aside.

In a large mixer bowl, combine flour, remaining cup of sugar, baking powder, salt, nutmeg, ginger, cloves, allspice and cinnamon.

Blend together egg yolks, pumpkin, oil and water in a small bowl; add to dry ingredients and beat just until smooth. Fold egg whites into batter until no white streaks remain. If mixer bowl is oven proof, simply scrape down sides of bowl and place in oven to bake. Otherwise pour batter into ungreased three-litre bowl. (Bowl should be eight to nine inches wide and about four inches deep).

Bake at 325 degrees F for 70 to 75 minutes or until cake tests done. Invert cake over wire rack to cool 15 to 20 minutes before removing from bowl. Cool on rack.

Frosting: Combine egg whites, sugar, corn syrup, water, cream of tartar and salt in a double boiler. Set over rapidly boiling water. Water should not touch bottom of top pan. Beat with an electric mixer on high until the mixture will stand in stiff peaks (about five to seven minutes).

Place one-half cup frosting in each of two bowls. Tint remaining frosting orange with a few drops of yellow and red food coloring. Tint one small bowl green.

Combine icing sugar and cocoa and stir into frosting in other small bowl. Add more icing sugar if necessary to make frosting stiff enough to roll for eyes, nose and mouth.

Place cake on serving plate; cover with orange frosting. Make long deep swirls to resemble pumpkin shape. Cut three inches from stem-end of banana. Place banana on top of cake and frost with green frosting. Spread remaining green frosting around base of banana to indicate base of stem.

Put chocolate icing on a piece of aluminum foil and using a dampened rolling pin, roll frosting to one-quarter inch thickness.Cut triangles for eyes and nose and a generous crescent for mouth. Put these pieces in refrigerator to set, then press onto side of cake to make face. You may have to do more shaping with your fingers.

Wacky Cake

This is a great recipe for beginner cooks as it is always successful, is fun to make and there is a minimum of clean-up after the preparation — only the measuring utensils.

The cake is very moist, keeps well, travels well and seems to get even better a day after baking. The recipe does not use milk or eggs, which is a bonus for some allergy sufferers. It doesn't get any easier than this.

Makes 9-inch square pan

3 cups all purpose flour
2 cups sugar
1/2 cup cocoa
2 tsp. baking soda
1 tsp. salt
2 tbsp. vinegar
2 tsp. vanilla
2/3 cup salad oil
2 cups water
1/2 cup chopped nuts (optional)

Sift flour, sugar, cocoa, soda and salt together into ungreased nine-inch square pan. Make three equally spaced holes in the flour mixture. Pour vinegar into one, vanilla into another and oil into the third. Gently pour water over top and stir well until all ingredients are thoroughly blended. Stir in nuts if desired.

Bake at 350 degrees for 30 to 35 minutes. Cool and ice, or sprinkle lightly with icing sugar. Serve plain or with ice cream or fruit.

Angel Cream Pavlova

Anna Pavlova, a famous Russian ballerina, had a delectable dessert named in her honor. The shell is a meringue, crispy on the outside and soft inside. It can be filled with a creamy filling or fresh fruit.

Although wonderful anytime, it has become our traditional Easter dessert.

6 - 8 servings

Pavlova:

3 egg whites
3/4 cup sugar
1/2 tsp. cornstarch
1/2 tsp. vinegar
1/2 tsp. vanilla
Cornstarch

Filling:

4 egg yolks
1/3 cup sugar
3 tbsp. lemon juice
Grated rind of 1 lemon
250 mL whipping cream, whipped

Pavlova: Whip egg whites until stiff. Add sugar, one tablespoon at a time, beating well after each addition. It should take 15 to 20 minutes to add sugar. Add cornstarch with last amount of sugar then beat in vinegar and vanilla.

Draw a nine- or 10-inch circle on a piece of brown, parchment or wax paper. Oil lightly and sprinkle with cornstarch. Spread meringue on circle; build up sides with back of spoon and hollow the centre. Leave at least one-quarter inch on bottom of meringue when hollowing out the centre. Bake at 300 degrees F for one hour or at 200 degrees F for two to 2 1/2 hours, until crisp and dry. Open oven door and let meringue cool thoroughly. Very gently peel away paper.

Filling: Combine egg yolks, sugar, lemon juice and rind in top of double boiler. Cook until thickened. Cool completely with wax paper pressed to surface to prevent a skin forming. Fold in whipped cream. Do not fill meringue until just before serving. Filling may be doubled.

Alternative to cream filling: 250 mL whipping cream, 2 to 3 tbsp. icing sugar and 1/2 tsp. vanilla. Whip cream, add sugar and vanilla. Spread into centre of meringue; top with pureed apricots and sliced kiwi fruit.

Elderberry Pie

Makes 9-inch pie

Pastry for a 2-crust pie
4 - 5 tbsp. all purpose flour*
3/4 cup sugar
1/2 tsp. cinnamon (optional)
Dash salt
4 - 5 cups frozen or fresh elderberries*
1 tbsp. margarine or butter

*Use 5 tbsp. flour if elderberries have been frozen. Partially thaw frozen berries in a sieve to allow extra liquid to drain away.

Roll out one-half of pastry and line nine-inch pie plate.

Combine flour, sugar, cinnamon, if used, and salt; sprinkle about one-quarter of this mixture over bottom pie crust. Add remainder of flour mixture to elderberries and toss to mix well. Fill pie shell with berries; dot with margarine.

Roll out remaining pastry for top crust. Seal edges and flute. Cut small vents in top crust.

Bake pie at 400 degrees F for 15 minutes. Reduce heat to 350 degrees F and bake another 30 to 35 minutes, or until top is lightly browned and filling is bubbling. (It may be necessary to place a cookie sheet on lower rack to catch boil-overs).

Irish Coffee Pie

A little bite of heaven!

6 - 8 servings

1 9-inch pie shell, baked and cooled
1 package (92 g) vanilla instant pudding
2 tsp. instant coffee granules
1/2 cup cold milk
1/3 cup water
3 tbsp. Irish Whisky
250 mL whipping cream, whipped stiff
Chocolate shavings*

***To shave chocolate:** Hold a wrapped square of unsweetened chocolate in the hand to warm it slightly. Unwrap and shave chocolate with long thin strokes using a vegetable peeler. If chocolate breaks, it is still too cold. Shave chocolate over waxed paper, then gently shake paper over pie.

In mixing bowl, blend together pudding mix, coffee and milk. Beat on high speed with electric mixer until fluffy, about one minute. Add water and whisky and beat on high speed for two minutes. Fold in all the whipped cream except a few tablespoons to be used as a garnish.

Fill pie shell with pudding mixture; chill until firm. Garnish with reserved whipped cream and chocolate shavings.

Jean's Strawberry Devonshire Tart

It is traditional to top this pie with whipped cream although we believe the true flavor of the strawberries is masked by it.

Makes 9-inch pie

9-inch pastry shell, baked and cooled
125 g cream cheese, softened
3 tbsp. sour cream or yogurt
1½ quarts fresh strawberries
3 tbsp. cornstarch
½ cup water
1 cup sugar
¼ tsp. almond extract

Beat cream cheese with electric mixer until fluffy and light; add sour cream and mix thoroughly. Spread mixture over bottom of pie shell.

Wash and hull berries and pat dry. Mash one quart of berries to make one cup puree. In a saucepan stir cornstarch and water together; add sugar and puree. Cook over medium heat, stirring constantly until mixture is clear and thickened; boil one minute longer. Stir in almond extract and stir frequently while cooling. Blend mixture in blender if you desire a smoother gel.

Arrange remaining whole berries, tips up, on cheese layer in pie shell. Pour cooled berry mixture evenly and carefully over berries. Chill pie a few hours before serving. Top with whipped cream if desired.

Tiny Tarts With Lemon Filling

Makes 2 cups; fills 40 tiny tart shells

Mini tart shells, baked and cooled
1¼ cups sugar
Juice of 2 large lemons
Grated rind of 1 lemon
2 eggs, beaten
1 tbsp. butter

Combine sugar, lemon juice and rind in the top of a double boiler. Cook over gently boiling water until clear, stirring constantly. Add a small amount of hot mixture to eggs and stir. Gradually return eggs to lemon mixture; cook until thick, stirring often. Remove from heat and add butter; stir to melt and mix. Cool and refrigerate. Use to fill tiny tart shells; filling is also good in layer cake or spread on toast.

Pat's Dutch Apple Pie

It took me a long time to duplicate this recipe as my mother put in "a little of this and a handful of that." She insisted that commercial sour cream is too thick and so you must "sour" fresh cream.

Makes 9-inch pie

1 unbaked 9-inch pie shell
5 to 6 tart cooking apples
Salt
2 tbsp. flour
1 1/3 cups brown sugar
3/4 tsp. cinnamon
2/3 cup soured cream (18% MF)*

*Cream may be soured by adding one tablespoon lemon juice or vinegar to two-thirds cup cream.

Peel and core apples; cut into quarters, sixths or eighths, depending on the size of the apples. Arrange apples in pie shell, rounded side up; sprinkle with salt.

Mix the flour, sugar and cinnamon and sprinkle evenly over the apples. Pour cream over all.

Bake at 400 degrees F for 15 minutes; reduce temperature to 350 degrees F, and bake 30 to 45 minutes longer, or until apples are tender.

This pie is best served warm. It can be reheated.

Rhubarb Cream Pie

Rhubarb has lots of uses of course, but tastes so good in pies that at one time it was called "pie plant."

Makes 9-inch pie

1 unbaked 9-inch pie crust
3/4 cup sugar
1/2 cup brown sugar
1/4 cup all purpose flour
1/2 tsp. nutmeg (optional)
1 egg, well beaten
1/2 cup sour cream or yogurt
4 cups diced rhubarb

Streusel Topping:

1/2 cup brown sugar
1/2 cup whole wheat flour
1/4 cup butter or margarine

Stir together sugars, flour and nutmeg (if used). Add egg and sour cream; beat until smooth. Arrange rhubarb in pastry shell; pour egg mixture over.

Topping: Mix brown sugar and whole wheat flour in a medium bowl. Cut in butter until mixture has a crumbly texture; sprinkle over filling.

Bake pie at 450 degrees F for 10 to 15 minutes; reduce temperature to 350 degrees F and continue baking for about 35 minutes, or until rhubarb is tender and topping is browned.

Fresh Cherry Pie

Makes 9-inch pie

Pastry for a 2-crust pie
1/2 cup sugar
1/2 cup brown sugar
3 tbsp. flour
3 1/2 cups pitted sour cherries (not frozen or thawed)
2 - 3 tsp. butter or margarine
1/4 tsp. almond flavoring

In mixing bowl, stir sugars and flour together; mix in cherries. Put cherry mixture in pastry lined pie pan and dot with butter. Drizzle flavoring over filling. Cover pie with a lattice pastry top; bake in a preheated oven at 350 degrees F for 45 to 55 minutes.

COOKIES & SQUARES

Anise Crescents

Not only are these licorice-flavored cookies delicious, but they are also a boon to those who are allergic to eggs or on low cholesterol diets.

Makes about 3 dozen

2 cups all purpose flour
1/4 cup finely chopped nuts*
1 tbsp. anise seed
1/2 tsp. salt
3/4 cup vegetable oil
3/4 cup icing sugar
2 tbsp. orange juice
1/2 tsp. vanilla

*Chop the nuts very fine, otherwise it is difficult to shape the cookies.

Stir together flour, nuts, anise seed and salt in a medium bowl. Add oil and stir until well blended. Mix together sugar, orange juice and vanilla and add to flour mixture; mix well. (Mixture will be crumbly.) Shape dough into rolls about two inches long and three-quarter inch in diameter. Curve into crescent shape and place on ungreased cookie sheet.

Bake at 350 degrees F for 20 to 22 minutes or until lightly browned.

Eggless Pumpkin Cookies

This soft cookie offers a nutritious balance often difficult to achieve — the pumpkin supplies Vitamin A and the wheat germ, Vitamin B.

Makes 5 dozen

1 can (14 oz./398 mL) canned pumpkin
3/4 cup brown sugar
3/4 cup vegetable oil
1/4 cup honey
1 1/2 tsp. vanilla
3 1/3 cups all purpose flour
1/2 cup wheat germ
2 tsp. baking powder
1 1/2 tsp. baking soda
2 tsp. cinnamon
1/2 tsp. each of nutmeg, ginger, allspice and salt
1/2 cup chopped raisins
1/3 cup chopped nuts (optional)

Stir pumpkin, sugar, oil, honey and vanilla together. Put flour, wheat germ, baking powder, baking soda, cinnamon, nutmeg, ginger, allspice and salt in a large mixing bowl and stir to combine. Add liquid ingredients to dry, and mix thoroughly; stir in raisins, and nuts, if used.

Drop batter from a teaspoon onto greased cookie sheets and bake at 350 degrees F for 10 minutes. Let cookies stand on baking sheet before moving to wire racks to cool; store in covered container in refrigerator.

Chicken Bones

Makes a nice Christmas gift!

Makes 16 - 18 cookies

2 - 3 squares semi-sweet chocolate OR about 1/3 cup chocolate chips
1 tsp. paraffin wax*
1 cup icing sugar
1/3 cup peanut butter
2 tbsp. butter, melted
1/4 cup Kellogg's Rice Krispies**
Finely chopped nuts or coconut

* The wax adds gloss to the chocolate. Paraffin wax is a "permitted" additive in Canada and we don't feel that this small amount is a health risk, but if you have concerns about adding a petro-chemical product to your food, omit it.

** Registered trademark of Kellogg Canada Inc.

Melt chocolate and wax in double-boiler. While chocolate is melting, combine sugar, peanut butter and butter in a separate bowl. Stir in cereal.

Mixture must be squeezed together with your hands.

To form cookies, squeeze pieces of the mixture into small logs. These will be uneven and perhaps show finger indentations. Form all of the logs first, then roll logs in melted chocolate. With two spoons, turn logs to coat, then remove and drop onto chopped nuts or coconut. Turn to coat, then set aside on waxed paper to harden. Store chicken bones in tightly covered container in the refrigerator.

These cookies are so good we are sure you will want to double the batch.

Man-size Chocolate Chip Cookies

Baking cookies can be fun and creative — you can often substitute flavorings and other ingredients to change your basic recipe. For example, you can substitute one teaspoon almond flavoring for the vanilla in these cookies. Or you can use pecans, almonds, walnuts, filberts or peanuts, or increase the nuts to one cup. Some people prefer raisins to nuts in cookies. Just be sure that dried fruits are well mixed into the batter and watch the baking time carefully, as they are more likely to burn than nuts or other ingredients.

4 dozen

3/4 cup shortening, at room temperature
3/4 cup margarine or butter, at room temperature
2/3 cup sugar
1 cup brown sugar
2 eggs
2 tsp. vanilla extract
3 cups all purpose flour
1 tsp. baking powder
1/2 tsp. salt
1/2 cup chopped nuts
350 g chocolate chips (2 cups)

Cream shortening and margarine thoroughly with sugars; beat in eggs and vanilla.

Stir flour, baking powder and salt together and add to creamed mixture, along with nuts and chocolate chips. Stir by hand, or use lowest speed on mixer, just until dough is well blended.

Drop heaping tablespoonfuls of dough onto ungreased cookie sheets, about two inches apart.

Bake at 375 degrees F for eight to 10 minutes, or until lightly browned. Let cool one to two minutes before removing from cookie sheet to wire rack or heavy paper to cool completely.

Krispie Cookies

Makes 6 dozen

2 1/2 cups all purpose flour
1 tsp. baking soda
1/2 tsp. salt
1 cup butter, softened
2 cups sugar
2 eggs
2 tsp. vanilla
4 cups Kellogg's Rice Krispies*
1 cup chocolate chips

*Registered Trademark of Kellogg Canada Inc.

Stir flour, baking soda and salt together. In a separate bowl, cream butter and sugar with electric mixer; add eggs and vanilla. Slowly beat in flour mixture. Fold in (do not use electric beater) Rice Krispies* and chocolate chips.

Drop from a teaspoon onto greased cookie sheets. Bake at 350 degrees F for 10 to 12 minutes.

Rum Balls

Rum balls are a good way to use stale cake crumbs or broken cookies.

Makes about 24

2 tbsp. unsweetened cocoa
1 cup icing sugar
1/4 cup rum
2 tbsp. corn syrup
2 cups finely crushed vanilla wafers or other cookie crumbs
1 cup finely chopped walnuts or pecans
2 tbsp. icing sugar, second amount

In a medium bowl mix cocoa and icing sugar together. Add rum and corn syrup and mix well. Add cookie crumbs and nuts; mix well, using fingers when mixture becomes too hard to stir.

Form mixture into one to 1 1/2 inch balls and roll in icing sugar. Allow cookies to stand, covered with a tea towel overnight before storing in an airtight container.

Apple-Date Meringue Squares

Makes 8- or 9-inch square pan

Filling:

- **1/2 cup chopped dates**
- **1/2 cup chopped apple**
- **1/2 cup apple juice**

Meringue:

- **2 egg whites**
- **1/4 tsp. cream of tartar**
- **1/3 cup sugar**
- **1 1/2 cups desiccated coconut**

Base:

- **1 3/4 cups cake and pastry flour**
- **1 tsp. baking powder**
- **1/2 cup butter or margarine**
- **1/2 cup sugar**
- **2 egg yolks**
- **1 tsp. vanilla**

Make filling first: Combine dates, apples and juice. Heat to boiling; simmer until thickened and soft, stirring frequently. Cool.

Grease an 8- or 9-inch square cake pan.

Meringue: Beat egg whites and cream of tartar to form soft peaks. Gradually beat in one-third cup sugar until whites are stiff and glossy; fold in coconut. Set meringue aside.

Base: Sift flour before measuring, then measure and stir or sift flour and baking powder together; set aside. Cream butter and sugar together; add egg yolks and vanilla, beat until light and fluffy. Stir in dry ingredients. Press mixture into prepared pan. Cover base with filling. Spread the meringue over filling.

Bake at 350 degrees F for 40 to 45 minutes.

When cool, cut into squares.

Back Packer's Delight

The combination of cereal, whole wheat flour, wheat germ, dried fruit, nuts and eggs in these squares provides vitamins, minerals, protein, simple and complex carbohydrates as well as dietary fibre. They are high in calories, but not "empty" calories.

Makes 9 by 13 inch pan, 24 - 32 squares

1 cup butter or margarine, softened
1¼ cups brown sugar, divided
5 eggs
2 cups bran flakes
1 cup whole wheat flour
½ cup wheat germ
Grated rind of one orange
1½ cups coarsely chopped unblanched almonds
½ cup chopped dates
1 cup chopped dried apricots
½ cup flaked coconut

Cream butter and one cup sugar together; beat in one egg. Add bran flakes, flour, wheat germ and orange rind and mix well. Spread mixture evenly in a 9 by 13 inch pan. (There is enough to cover the bottom of the pan, but you will have to use your hands or the flat surface of a spatula to do so.)

Mix almonds, dates, apricots and coconut together; sprinkle evenly over cereal layer.

Combine remaining eggs and brown sugar; mix well. Pour over fruit and nuts, tilting pan if necessary to ensure that all the fruit mixture is moistened with egg mixture.

Bake at 350 degrees F for about 30 minutes, or until topping is set and golden brown.

Cool completely. Cut into squares or bars. Store in airtight container.

Chocolate-Orange Brownies

Do you know anyone who doesn't like brownies? When Pat lived in London, England, many years ago, her standard dessert or tea time treat for visitors was brownies — a novel North American invention.

These cake-type brownies team chocolate with one of its many compatible flavors — orange.

Makes 8 or 9 inch square pan

1/2 cup shortening or margarine
3/4 cup sugar
2 eggs
2 squares (28 g each) unsweetened chocolate, melted
Grated rind of 1 orange
3/4 cup chopped nuts (optional)
1 1/3 cups all purpose flour
1 1/2 tsp. baking powder
1/4 tsp. salt
1/2 cup milk

Glaze:

1/2 cup icing sugar
2 tbsp. orange juice

Grease and flour an 8 or 9-inch square baking pan.

Cream shortening and sugar together until light and fluffy. Add eggs and beat well. Stir or beat in chocolate, orange rind and nuts if used.

Stir flour, baking powder and salt together; add alternately with milk to creamed mixture. Stir just until blended.

Pour batter into prepared pan and bake at 350 degrees F (325 degrees F if using a glass pan) for 30 to 35 minutes.

Glaze: Combine icing sugar and orange juice in a small bowl or glass measure. Set in a warm place (near the oven vent is a good place) while brownies bake, stirring occasionally.

Pour glaze over hot brownies. Let cool in pan; cut into squares.

Creme de Menthe Bars

Makes 36 - 40 bars

Base:

2 squares (28 g each) unsweetened chocolate
1/2 cup butter or margarine
1/2 cup sugar
1/2 cup brown sugar
2 eggs
1 tsp. vanilla (optional)
2/3 cup all purpose flour
1/2 tsp. baking powder

Filling:

1/2 cup butter or margarine, softened
2 cups icing sugar
2 tbsp. green creme de menthe liqueur
1/4 tsp. peppermint extract

Topping:

1 cup semi-sweet chocolate pieces*
2 tbsp. vegetable oil or butter

*For the topping, you could substitute two squares unsweetened chocolate for the semi-sweet chips and reduce oil to one tablespoon.

Base: Combine unsweetened chocolate and butter in a medium saucepan or top of double boiler; melt over low heat or hot water. Stir until smooth. Blend in sugars; beat in eggs and vanilla, if used. Combine flour and baking powder and stir into chocolate mixture.

Spread batter in a greased 7 by 11 inch pan or 9-inch square pan and bake at 350 degrees F for 20 to 25 minutes. (Don't over-cook the base; the texture should be like fudgy brownies and it may even fall slightly while cooling.) Cool completely.

Filling: In a small mixing bowl, cream butter; beat in icing sugar. Add creme de menthe and peppermint extract; beat until smooth and creamy. Spread filling over cooled base; refrigerate until set.

Topping: Combine chocolate chips and oil in small saucepan or top of double boiler. Cook over low heat or hot water until chocolate is melted. Stir until smooth; spread over chilled filling. Refrigerate to set.

Store bars in the refrigerator, but allow to stand at room temperature for 10 minutes before cutting into bars or squares (to prevent cracking the chocolate topping).

Mincemeat-Coconut Bars

Great for company or gift giving.

Makes 1½ - 2 dozen

Base:

1½ cups quick cooking rolled oats
1¼ cups all purpose flour
1 tsp. baking soda
⅓ cup brown sugar
¾ cup butter or margarine at room temperature

Topping:

1 egg
3 tbsp. sugar
1 package (4-serving size) vanilla pudding and pie filling mix*
½ tsp. baking powder
½ cup evaporated milk
1⅓ cups flaked coconut
1 cup mincemeat

*Not instant pudding.

Base: Combine oats, flour, baking soda and brown sugar in a medium bowl. Cut in butter with a pastry blender or two knives. Reserve one cup oatmeal mixture; press remainder evenly in bottom of a greased 11 by 7 inch pan or 9-inch square pan.

Bake at 350 degrees F for 15 minutes.

Topping: Beat egg in medium bowl; gradually beat in sugar. Stir in pudding mix, baking powder, evaporated milk, coconut and mince-meat.

Spread filling mixture over baked base; sprinkle reserved oatmeal mixture over filling.

Bake at 350 degrees F for 30 minutes. Cool completely, then cut into bars.

Old-Fashioned Oatmeal Treats

Simple, "homey" recipes — just like Mom made — are called "comfort" foods because they remind us of the days when Mom could resolve all our problems with a kiss and a cookie.

Surprisingly enough, some old-fashioned recipes seem modern because they are quick and easy to prepare and/or they contain ingredients that we now value for their nutrients.

These oatmeal squares are very basic, easy and good tasting. Like most cookies, they are relatively high in fat and should be eaten in moderation. These have the advantage of being made primarily with whole grains instead of refined flour and are not too sweet.

We like these simple squares served with another homey food, fresh-from-the-garden stewed rhubarb.

Makes 2 dozen squares

3 1/2 cups quick cooking rolled oats
2/3 cup brown sugar
1/4 cup all purpose flour
1/4 tsp. salt
3/4 cup butter, at room temperature*
1 tsp. vanilla extract

* In a recipe with so few ingredients, the flavor of the fat is important. You may substitute margarine for some of the butter, but don't replace it all.

In a large mixing bowl, combine oats, sugar, flour and salt; stir well. Add butter and vanilla, working the butter into the dry ingredients with your fingers or a wooden spoon, until the mixture is crumbly and well blended.

Press the dough into a well-greased 7 by 11 inch pan, or 9-inch square pan. Bake at 350 degrees F for 15 to 18 minutes, or until top is golden and "toasty".

Cool completely in pan before cutting into squares or bars.

BREADS & MUFFINS

Buttermilk Rolls

The use of buttermilk as a liquid in baking, produces a very tender and tasty product. Baking soda is always added when buttermilk is present to neutralize its acid and to prevent the product from tasting sour. For that reason, this recipe contains baking soda as well as yeast.

Makes 2 dozen

2 cups buttermilk
1/4 cup margarine or butter, melted
5 cups all purpose flour
1 envelope quick rise or 1 tbsp. instant yeast
3 tbsp. sugar
1 tsp. salt
1/2 tsp. baking soda

Heat buttermilk to 125 to 130 degrees F (use temperature probe in your microwave, if you have one); add to melted margarine.

Place four cups of the flour in a large mixing bowl, add yeast, sugar, salt and baking soda and mix well. Stir in hot liquids and mix thoroughly. Continue to mix, working in remaining flour until dough is soft but not sticky. (You may do this last part on a floured surface instead of in the bowl.)

Cover dough with a clean tea towel and let rest 10 minutes.

Grease two eight-inch square pans. Turn dough onto a lightly floured surface, punch down and knead about one minute.

Divide dough in half; cut each half into 12 equal parts. Shape into balls and place 12 in each pan. Cover and let rise in draft-free place until double in size (30 to 60 minutes).

Bake at 400 degrees F for 15 to 20 minutes or until golden brown. If rolls begin to brown too much, cover loosely with foil.

To make cloverleaf rolls, divide each portion into three and form into balls. Place three balls of dough in each section of well oiled muffin tins, let rise and bake for 12 to 15 minutes.

Hearty Multi-Grain Bread

There is a wonderful variety of textures and flavors possible in homemade breads; this one is dark and hearty with a robust flavor.

Makes 2 loaves

- **2 cups milk**
- **1 cup water**
- **2 cups quick-cooking oats**
- **$^1/_4$ cup shortening**
- **$^1/_4$ cup molasses**
- **$^1/_4$ cup brown sugar**
- **2 tsp. salt**
- **2 tbsp. instant yeast**
- **2 cups whole wheat flour**
- **$1^1/_2$ cups dark rye flour**
- **$2^1/_2$ to 3 cups all purpose flour**

Heat milk and water almost to boiling (the high temperature helps to soften the oats and melt the shortening quickly).

In a large glass mixing bowl, combine oats, shortening, molasses, sugar and salt. Add hot liquid and stir until shortening is melted. Cool to lukewarm.

Stir instant yeast into cooled oatmeal mixture. Beat in whole-wheat flour, mixing well. Stir in rye flour. Gradually add sufficient all purpose flour to make a smooth, fairly stiff dough. Remove dough to a floured board and work in more flour as you knead it. Knead until dough is no longer sticky — about 10 minutes. Form dough into a ball.

Wash mixing bowl in hot water; dry and rub with shortening or oil. Place dough in bowl and rotate dough to coat it with the shortening. Cover bowl with greased wax paper and a warm damp tea towel. Place in microwave oven and set it at 10% power (more than 100 watts of microwave energy will kill the yeast before it has a chance to rise.) Let dough rise until doubled in bulk — 20 to 25 minutes. (This will take about 75 minutes in a warm, draft-free place.)

Punch dough down and cut in half; shape into round or oval loaves and place each in well-greased 1.5-litre microwavable and oven-proof casseroles (for example, Pyrex). Recover pans with greased wax paper and warm damp cloth and let rise at 10% power for 18 to 20 minutes, or until almost doubled in bulk (about one hour in warm place).

Meanwhile, preheat conventional oven to 375 degrees F. Bake bread for 15 minutes; reduce temperature to 350 degrees F and bake for 40 to 45 minutes, or until bread leaves sides of pans. When done, bread should come out of the pan easily and will sound hollow when tapped lightly with the knuckles.

Whole Wheat Bread Sticks

Soft on the inside and crusty on the outside, homemade bread sticks are as unlike the perfectly formed commercial ones as any hand-crafted article is unlike its factory made counterpart. Serve them with a meal or pack them with a salad or veggies for brown bag lunches.

2 - $2\frac{1}{2}$ dozen

$2\frac{1}{2}$ cups whole wheat flour
$\frac{1}{2}$ cup natural wheat bran
1 tbsp. instant yeast OR 1 envelope active dry yeast
$\frac{1}{2}$ tsp. salt
$1\frac{1}{4}$ cups water
$\frac{1}{4}$ cup butter or margarine
2 tbsp. honey
$\frac{1}{2}$ cup broken or chopped sunflower seeds
1 egg yolk
1 tbsp. milk

In large mixer bowl, stir together two cups flour, bran, yeast and salt.

Combine water, butter and honey in a four-cup glass measure (or small saucepan) and heat until very warm (120 to 130 degrees F). Use the temperature probe in your microwave if you have one, otherwise heat mixture about $1\frac{1}{2}$ minutes at 50% (Medium or Medium-Low) power. Slowly add warm liquid to dry ingredients.

Beat dough two minutes at medium speed; remove beaters. Add remaining flour and stir vigorously until all is incorporated.

On a well floured surface, knead dough five minutes. Knead in sunflower seeds and remaining flour; continue kneading until dough is elastic and no longer sticky (another three to five minutes).

Put dough into a warmed, greased microwavable bowl, turning dough around and over to grease all sides. Cover loosely with wax paper and then with a dampened tea towel. Let rise in microwave oven at 10% power for 18 to 20 minutes, or until doubled in bulk. (Set in a warm place for about 40 minutes if your microwave oven doesn't have this very low setting).

Cut dough in half and roll each half into a "log." Cut each log into 12 or 15 pieces and shape each piece into a six to eight inch stick. Place bread sticks on greased cookie sheets, one to two inches apart. Cover again with greased wax paper and let rise 30 minutes in a warm place.

Lightly beat egg yolk and milk together; brush over bread sticks. Bake at 400 degrees F for 15 minutes or until brown and crusty. Remove from pans and cool on wire racks.

Irish Soda Bread

This quick and easy bread is more like a giant scone than a traditional loaf of bread. The dough is softer than yeast dough.

Irish soda bread smells and tastes wonderful; it can be served plain or taosted. The honey helps to keep the bread fresh and tender.

Makes 1 round loaf

2 cups whole wheat flour*
1/2 tsp. salt
1 tsp. baking soda
1 egg, beaten
1 tbsp. liquid honey
1 cup yogurt (or buttermilk)
1 tbsp. melted butter or margarine

*Stir, but do not sift flour before measuring.

Grease a small cookie sheet and set aside.

In a large mixing bowl, stir together flour, salt and baking soda.

In a medium bowl, combine egg, honey and yogurt; add liquids to dry ingredients and stir until dry ingredients are just moistened.

Place dough on a well floured work surface; knead gently until smooth (five minutes or less), working in a little more flour if necessary. Shape dough into a flat round ball about seven inches in diameter on cookie sheet.

With a large, floured knife, make about a four-inch slash into centre of loaf, almost through to bottom.

Repeat at right angles. (This allows steam to escape.)

Bake at 375 degrees F for 35 to 40 minutes, or until top is browned and loaf sounds hollow when tapped. Brush top with butter. Cool on wire rack.

Yogurt and Blueberry Muffins

Muffins are quick and easy to make, and can be very nutritious. They make an excellent breakfast food — especially tempting for picky eaters. This recipe uses yogurt, which accounts for their delicate flavor and texture.

12 large or 18 medium

2 1/2 cups all purpose flour
3/4 cup sugar
2 tsp. baking powder
1 tsp. baking soda
1/2 tsp. salt
1/2 cup butter or margarine
1 cup plain yogurt
2 eggs
Grated rind of one orange
1 cup fresh or frozen blueberries

Mix flour, sugar, baking powder, baking soda and salt together. Cut butter in until mixture resembles coarse crumbs. Lightly beat yogurt and eggs together, then add all at once to dry ingredients.

Stir just to moisten the dry ingredients. Fold in orange rind and blueberries. Spoon batter into greased muffin cups. Bake at 400 degrees F for 15 to 20 minutes or until a toothpick comes out clean. Large muffins will take the longer time to bake. Serve warm and fresh from the oven.

> **Note:** If you intend to serve muffins the same day they are baked, we advise you not to use muffin papers because too much of the muffin adheres to the paper. Just grease the muffin pans instead.

Fanfare Muffins

For 40 summers, a trumpet fanfare has called people to their seats at the Stratford Festival. This muffin recipe was sent to us from the Fanfare Book Store in Stratford, Ont., many years ago and we are pleased to share it with you.

Makes 2 dozen

3/4 cup All Bran* cereal
1/2 cup rye flakes**
1/2 cup rolled oats
1 can (160 mL) or 2/3 cup evaporated milk
1 cup milk
1 1/4 cups whole wheat flour
1 cup brown sugar
1 tsp. baking powder
1/2 tsp. baking soda
1 tsp. salt
1 1/2 cups raisins
1/2 cup sunflower seeds
1/4 cup wheat germ
2 eggs
2 tsp. vanilla extract
1 ripe banana, mashed
1/2 cup vegetable oil

*Registered trademark of Kellogg Canada Inc.

**You may have to purchase rye flakes in a natural food store.

Combine All Bran*, rye flakes and rolled oats in a medium bowl; pour evaporated milk and milk over cereals and let stand several minutes to moisten cereals.

Grease 24 medium muffin cups.

Thoroughly combine flour, sugar, baking powder, baking soda, salt, raisins, sunflower seeds and wheat germ in a large mixing bowl.

In a smaller bowl, beat together the eggs, vanilla, mashed banana and oil. Combine liquid ingredients with cereal mixture, then stir into dry ingredients, just until mixed.

Fill prepared muffin cups three-quarters full and bake at 350 degrees F for 20 minutes, or until lightly browned and batter does not stick to a toothpick inserted into the centre of a muffin.

Ila's Bran Muffins

These muffins were always a favorite during the many years that Ila Hoffman cooked at the Rockway Golf Club in Kitchener.

Makes 10 - 12

1 egg
1/2 cup vegetable oil
1 cup brown sugar
1/2 cup sour cream
2 cups natural wheat bran
1 cup all purpose flour
1 tsp. baking soda
1 tsp. baking powder
Pinch salt
1/3 cup boiling water

In a large mixing bowl, beat together egg, oil, sugar and sour cream. Stir in bran and mix until well moistened.

Stir together flour, baking soda, baking powder and salt; add to bran mixture and stir just until blended. Stir in boiling water and immediately spoon batter into prepared (greased or paper lined) muffin cups and bake at 375 degrees F for 15 to 20 minutes, or until done (a toothpick inserted in muffin comes out clean).

Oat Bran Muffins

Makes 12

1 1/2 cups all purpose flour
1 cup oat bran
2 tsp. baking powder
1/2 tsp. baking soda
1/4 cup chopped nuts
1/4 cup chopped dried fruit
1/3 cup brown sugar
1 cup skim or 1% milk
1 egg
1/4 cup vegetable oil

Combine flour, oat bran, baking powder, baking soda, nuts, dried fruit and sugar in a mixing bowl.

Whisk milk, egg and oil together, add to dry ingredients, stir just to mix. (Batter will be lumpy.) Fill greased muffin cups and bake at 400 degrees F for 15 to 20 minutes.

Seasoned breads

A slice of hot, crusty bread, mildly or wildly seasoned, is a great accompaniment to any meal — barbecued or otherwise.

RYE-HERB LOAF

The amounts of herbs given in this recipe are for dried herbs, except the parsley. If you grow your own fresh herbs, snip them finely and use three to four times as much.

8 - 9 servings

- **1/2 cup butter or margarine, softened**
- **1 clove garlic, pressed or finely minced**
- **1/4 tsp. freshly ground black pepper**
- **1/4 tsp. sage, crumbled**
- **1/4 tsp. rosemary**
- **1/4 tsp. thyme**
- **1/2 tsp. tarragon**
- **1/2 tsp. dry mustard**
- **3 tbsp. finely snipped fresh parsley or 1 tbsp. dried**
- **1 round loaf dark rye bread, sliced**

Combine butter, garlic, and all seasonings; mix well. Spread each slice of bread with seasoned butter. Reassemble loaf and wrap in heavy duty foil. Heat bread on upper rack of barbecue about 20 minutes or until heated through. Fold foil back to form a bread basket. Serve warm.

SESAME HERB BREAD

4 - 5 servings

- **1 small loaf French bread**
- **1/4 cup softened butter or margarine**
- **2 tbsp. snipped fresh parsley***
- **1/4 cup finely snipped fresh chives***
- **1 1/2 tbsp. toasted sesame seeds**

*If using dried herbs, use 1 1/2 to 2 teaspoons parsley and one tablespoon chives.

Slice bread diagonally into thick slices, without cutting through bottom crust. Combine butter, herbs and sesame seeds; spread on cut surfaces of bread.

Wrap loaf in heavy foil and heat on barbecue, 20 to 30 minutes, depending on temperature and distance from coals. If close to the coals, it is advisable to turn the loaf at least once. Or bake in oven at 350 degrees F for 25 to 30 minutes.

Sesame Crisps

Makes 18 - 24

6 slices bread
1/3 cup butter or margarine, melted
2 tbsp. toasted sesame seeds*

*You may also use caraway or poppy seeds or some of each.

Remove crusts from bread and cut each slice into three "fingers" or four triangles. Dip each piece into melted butter (or brush with melted butter) and sprinkle with toasted sesame seeds.

Place on a cookie sheet and toast in a preheated oven at 375 degrees F for 15 to 18 minutes or until brown and crisp. Serve hot with soup and/or salad.

To toast sesame seeds: Put seeds in small non-stick fry-pan and toast over medium heat; toss or stir until they are lightly and evenly browned.

Croutons

Makes about 1 1/2 cups

2 tbsp. butter or margarine
2 slices bread
Garlic powder or seasoning of your choice, if desired

To prepare croutons, melt butter in a heavy skillet over low heat. Trim crusts from bread and cut into quarter-inch or half-inch cubes.

Put cubes into skillet and toss until all sides are coated and browned. Sprinkle lightly with garlic powder while cooking, if desired.

Sour Cream Coffee Cake

You can make this light, tasty and attractive coffee cake the day before you serve it, so it is a good choice for brunch or anytime you have overnight visitors.

8 servings

Topping:

- **1/2 cup finely chopped nuts**
- **1/3 cup brown sugar**
- **1 tsp. cinnamon**

Batter:

- **1/2 cup butter or margarine**
- **3/4 cup sugar**
- **2 cups all purpose flour**
- **2 eggs**
- **1 cup sour cream (or plain yogurt)**
- **1 tsp. baking powder**
- **1 tsp. baking soda**
- **1 tsp. vanilla**

In small bowl, combine nuts, brown sugar and cinnamon; set aside.

In large mixing bowl, cream butter and sugar until light and fluffy. With mixer on low speed, mix in flour, then eggs, sour cream, baking powder, baking soda and vanilla; increase speed to medium once all the flour is well blended. Beat one to two minutes longer, scraping bowl with rubber spatula as needed.

Grease a nine-inch tube pan. Spread about half of the batter in pan; sprinkle with a generous layer of the nut mixture (use at least half of it). Add remaining batter and top with remaining nut mixture.

Bake at 350 degrees F for about one hour or until a skewer inserted in centre comes out clean.

Cool in pan 10 minutes, then invert onto serving plate. Serve warm or cold.

Pancake Pointers

The following tips apply to making pancakes from any recipe or from a mix.

- Cook pancakes on a griddle or in a skillet — electric or cast iron. Grease pan or not, as directed in recipe and according to type of pan.
- Griddle is hot enough when a few drops of water sprinkled over pan "bounce."
- Pancakes are ready to turn when tops are bubbly and edges look dry. The second side takes about half the cooking time of the first side.
- Stir waiting pancake batter several times or it will thicken.
- Pancakes are best eaten hot from the pan, but can be kept warm if necessary. Stack them on a warm plate, cover loosely with foil and place in a very low oven or over simmering water.
- Pancakes can be frozen. Separate cooled pancakes with wax paper and wrap for freezer storage. They can be reheated in a microwave or toaster oven.
- Unless otherwise specified, use about one-quarter cup batter per pancake. The following recipes provide two to three pancakes per serving.

Sour Cream Pancakes

The easiest possible pancake recipe.

8 - 9 pancakes

1 egg
2/3 cup sour cream
1/3 cup water
1 cup complete pancake mix (available at supermarket)

Heat griddle or frying pan over medium-high heat, to 350 degrees F if using electric frypan; grease lightly. Beat egg at high speed on electric mixer until thick and lemon colored; blend in sour cream and water.

Add pancake mix and mix until batter is fairly smooth. For each pancake, pour a scant one-quarter cup batter onto hot griddle. When tops are covered with bubbles and edges look cooked, turn pancakes over and cook until browned on bottom. Serve hot with syrup, applesauce or preserves.

Bill's Pancakes

Mix a large quantity of the dry ingredients to take to the cottage or on camping trips. Use one and three-quarter cups of the mix with the liquid ingredients for speedy pancakes.

About 10 pancakes

1 1/2 cups graham flour
3 tbsp. brown sugar
1 tbsp. baking powder
1 tsp. salt
1 1/3 cups milk
3 tbsp. melted butter or margarine
2 eggs, well beaten

Stir together flour, sugar, baking powder and salt. In mixing bowl, combine milk, melted butter and eggs. Add dry ingredients all at once to liquid ingredients. Stir quickly until ingredients are just mixed and batter is still lumpy.

Pour batter onto hot, lightly greased griddle (use approximately one-quarter cup batter per pancake). Cook until bubbles break on the top of the pancake and the surface has lost its sheen and is just beginning to set. Turn and cook until browned on bottom. Serve hot.

Cottage Cheese Pancakes

2 servings

2 eggs
3/4 cup small curd (or sieved) cottage cheese (1 or 2% M.F.)
1/4 cup light sour cream
1/2 tsp. sugar
1/4 tsp. salt
1/3 cup all purpose flour

In a medium bowl, beat eggs. Mix in cottage cheese, sour cream, sugar and salt and beat until all ingredients are well blended.

Sprinkle flour over cheese mixture and fold in. Preheat griddle or heavy skillet over medium-high heat (350 degrees F if using electric fry pan) and brush lightly with vegetable oil. Drop batter (about one-quarter cup per pancake) onto preheated griddle and cook pancakes until they are dry around the edges. Turn and cook other side. Serve immediately with topping of your choice.

Guilt-Free Pancakes

Ordinary pancakes, made with eggs and served with maple syrup, don't rate highly with nutritionists. We haven't eliminated the egg or all the fat from this pancake batter, but we did make the pancakes a better source of vitamins, minerals and fibre by using some whole wheat flour in the batter and topping the pancakes with sweetened yogurt and fruit.

4 - 5 servings

Fruit and Yogurt Topping:

- **1/2 cup low fat, plain yogurt**
- **2 tbsp. maple syrup**
- **2 cups fruit***

Whole Wheat Pancakes:

- **3/4 cup whole wheat flour**
- **1/2 cup all purpose flour**
- **2 tsp. baking powder**
- **1 1/2 tbsp. sugar**
- **1 egg, beaten**
- **1 1/4 cups skim milk**
- **1 - 2 tbsp. vegetable oil**

*When available, fresh blueberries, strawberries, raspberries, sliced peaches or papayas are wonderful toppings. Thawed, drained sliced peaches can also be used, and thinly sliced Poached Apples or Pears (see page 149) are also tasty.

Topping: Combine yogurt and maple syrup; mix well and set aside. Prepare fruit.

Pancakes: In mixing bowl, stir together flours, baking powder and sugar. Pour in egg, milk and oil; stir until dry ingredients are moistened (pancake batter does not have to be perfectly smooth). Let batter stand five minutes.

Heat a heavy, non-stick skillet over medium-high heat until hot. Set at 375 degrees if using an electric frying pan or test by sprinkling a few drops of water on pan. Grease pan very lightly. Using a quarter cup measure, drop batter onto hot skillet. Cook until surface of pancakes is covered with bubbles that start to break, and the edge of the pancake is set. Turn and cook on the other side until browned.

Serve immediately; spoon a little of the yogurt mixture over each pancake and top with fruit.

Wheat Germ and Raisin Pancakes

3 servings

Hot Lemon Syrup:

- **1/2 cup corn syrup**
- **3 tbsp. lemon juice**
- **2 tbsp. honey**
- **Grated rind of 1/2 lemon**

Pancakes:

- **3/4 cup all purpose flour**
- **1/2 cup wheat germ**
- **1 tsp. baking powder**
- **1/2 tsp. baking soda**
- **1/4 tsp. salt**
- **1 1/4 cups buttermilk (or soured milk)**
- **1 egg**
- **2 tbsp. vegetable oil**
- **1/4 cup raisins**

Syrup: To make syrup, combine corn syrup, lemon juice, honey and lemon rind. Boil until slightly thickened; keep warm.

Pancakes: Mix flour, wheat germ, baking powder, baking soda and salt. Beat buttermilk, egg and oil together; add to flour mixture and stir just until moistened. Stir in raisins.

Cook (about one-quarter cup batter for each pancake) on hot, lightly greased griddle, turn and cook bottom until lightly browned.

Serve with Hot Lemon Syrup.

Note: More syrup recipes are found on page 214.

PANTRY PROVISIONS

Antipasto

We like to make this in the fall when cauliflower is available. Some of the commercial products may not be available in the size listed, so, close counts!

Makes 8 500-mL jars

1 cup carrots*
1 cup sliced celery
1 small head of cauliflower, broken into flowerets
1 jar (375 mL) gherkins, drained and sliced
1 jar (375 mL) cocktail onions, drained
1 jar (250 mL) stuffed olives, drained and cut in thirds
1 can (10 oz./284 mL) button mushrooms, drained
1 L ketchup
3 bottles (300 mL each) chili sauce
1/2 cup horseradish
4 cans (6 1/2 oz./184 g each) flaked white tuna, drained
2 tbsp. white vinegar or lemon juice
2 tsp. Worcestershire sauce

*Use slender young carrots; cut into one-quarter inch thick slices.

Boil carrots and celery in a small amount of water for five minutes. Add the cauliflower and continue to cook another five to six minutes. (The vegetables should still be crunchy, to add texture to the anti-pasto.)

Drain vegetables and place in a very large mixing bowl or pot.

Add gherkins, onions, olives, mushrooms, ketchup, chili sauce, horse-radish, tuna, vinegar and Worcestershire sauce to the vegetables. Mix all ingredients together.

Pack mixture in sterile jars, being sure to distribute vegetables among the jars as evenly as possible. Keeps well in refrigerator or can be frozen.

For longer storage, cook antipasto for 10 to 15 minutes then pack into sterile jars, leaving one inch headspace. Process 15 minutes in a boiling water bath.

Serve with crackers as an appetizer.

Barbecue Spice

You can use this seasoning blend whenever "seasoned salt" or barbecue spice is called for. Fill a small bottle for immediate use and store the remainder in the freezer. Or put it into four or five small bottles and use as gifts.

Makes 1½ cups

6 tbsp. paprika
2 tbsp. brown sugar
2 tsp. curry powder
2 tsp. dry mustard
2 tsp. garlic salt
2 tsp. black pepper
2 tsp. onion powder
½ tsp. chili powder
½ tsp. nutmeg
½ tsp. dried thyme
½ tsp. dried tarragon
½ tsp. dried marjoram
½ tsp. dried basil
¼ tsp. cayenne
1 cup salt

Combine all ingredients in food processor or mixing bowl. With chopping blade in place, process until the herbs are pulverized and ingredients are well mixed. Or use the back of a spoon to powder herbs and stir to blend.

All Purpose Barbecue Sauce

Makes 1⅔ cups

¼ cup cider vinegar
⅓ - ½ cup water*
2 tbsp. sugar or corn syrup
1 tbsp. prepared mustard
1¼ tsp. Barbecue Spice (above)
1 thick slice lemon OR 2 slices lime
½ cooking onion, thinly sliced
¼ cup butter or margarine
½ cup ketchup
2 tbsp. Worcestershire sauce

*Use one-third cup water if cooking by microwave; one-half cup if simmering on stove.

Combine all ingredients except ketchup and Worcestershire sauce in a medium saucepan or a one-litre glass measure. Simmer, uncovered, for 20 minutes, stirring occasionally; OR cook on High power in microwave for two minutes; stir and cook at "Defrost" for seven to eight minutes, stir once. Add ketchup and Worcestershire sauce. Store in a covered jar in refrigerator.

Beef or Brown Stock

Makes about 8 cups

3 lb. beef bones
2 unpeeled onions
1 carrot, quartered
Water
2 ribs celery
$1^1/_2$ tsp. salt
1 tbsp. dried parsley
$^1/_2$ tsp. thyme
1 bay leaf

In roasting pan, roast bones at 450 degrees F for 30 minutes. Add onions and carrot and cook another 30 minutes at 400 degrees F. Transfer meat and vegetables to large stock pot or kettle. Pour off fat from roasting pan. Add two cups of water to pan and stir to deglaze; add to the stock pot along with 12 cups of water.

Bring to a boil; skim off froth. Add celery, salt, parsley, thyme and bay leaf and simmer four to six hours.

Remove bones and strain stock through a fine sieve. Let cool. Chill stock, then remove fat. Stock may be reduced further for more concentrated flavor. Stock may be frozen.

Cranberry Chutney

For best flavor results, make chutney at least two days before serving. It keeps well for several months and is great with poultry or ham.

Makes about 3 cups

2 cups cranberries
$^1/_2$ cup sugar*
1 can (14 oz./398 mL) apricot halves
$^1/_4$ cup chopped onion
1 tbsp. lemon juice
$^1/_2$ tsp. salt
Dash cayenne
$^1/_4$ tsp. ginger
$^1/_2$ cup raisins (optional)

*Use less sugar if apricots are packed in heavy syrup.

Wash berries and put in 1.5- to two-litre microwavable casserole; stir in sugar. Drain apricots well, saving syrup. Add syrup to cranberries along with onion, lemon juice, salt, cayenne, ginger and raisins, if used. Microwave on High power five to six minutes. Stir after two minutes.

Chop apricots and add to cranberries; cook on High another $1^1/_2$ to two minutes. Cool, bottle, then refrigerate.

Curried Fruit

This fruit dish adds pizzaz to your menu when served with ham, roast pork or poultry.

8 servings

1/4 cup butter or margarine
1/4 cup brown sugar
1 - 2 tsp. curry powder
1 large cooking apple, cored and cut in rings
1 can (14 oz./398 mL) pear halves, drained
1 can (14 oz./398 mL) peach slices or apricot halves,drained
1 can (14 oz./398 mL) unsweetened pineapple rings, drained
1/4 cup raisins

Melt butter in a small saucepan; stir in sugar and curry powder and heat to boiling.

Arrange fruit in a two-quart casserole (or a 7 inch by 11 inch baking dish) and pour hot curry sauce over it.

Bake, uncovered, at 325 degrees F for 30 to 35 minutes, or until thoroughly heated and apples are tender.

Spiced Prunes

Another different and delicious condiment to serve with either poultry or pork.

8 servings

1/2 lb. pitted prunes
2 cups cold water
1/4 cup vinegar
1/4 cup brown sugar
2 cinnamon sticks (4 inches long)
1 tsp. whole cloves

Soak prunes in water for eight hours or overnight. Place prunes and liquid in medium saucepan; add vinegar and sugar. Tie cinnamon and cloves in cheesecloth and add to prunes. Bring mixture to a boil; reduce heat and simmer for seven minutes.

Cool. Discard spice bag. Cover and chill 24 hours before serving. The spiced prunes will keep seven to 10 days in the refrigerator.

Eleanor's Basic Biscuit Mix

Homemade mix can be used in place of all purpose commercial biscuit mix for pancakes, dumplings, puddings, etc. It is a staple in our kitchens and is popular with our readers, too. This recipe appeared in our column several times over the years and always sparked many requests for recipes using the mix.

Makes about 13 cups

9 cups cake and pastry flour*
4 tbsp. baking powder
1 tbsp. salt
1 cup skim milk powder
1 lb. vegetable shortening

*You can substitute 8½ cups all purpose flour, or 4½ cups each of all purpose and whole wheat flours if you prefer. If using all purpose and whole wheat flours, increase baking powder to six tablespoons.

Sift cake and pastry flour before measuring, then sift the flour, baking powder, salt and milk powder together three times (once is sufficient if your sifter has three screens) into a very large mixing bowl.

Cut in shortening with a pastry blender or two knives until mixture resembles coarse crumbs.

Place biscuit mix in a large, air-tight container, label and date. Store mix in a cool, dry cupboard for two to three months. Freezer storage is recommended for storage longer than three months.

Easy Maple Flavored Syrup

Makes 2 cups

1 cup corn syrup
1/2 cup brown sugar
1/2 cup water
2 - 3 drops maple flavoring
1 tbsp. butter

Combine all ingredients in a medium saucepan; heat to boiling. Stirring constantly, boil for one minute. Remove from heat, stir in flavoring and butter. Store in clean glass jar in refrigerator. Shake well before using. Can be served warm or cold.

Mock Maple Syrup

A thinner syrup with a nice, light flavor.

Makes 1 cup

1 cup sugar
1 tbsp. brown sugar
1 cup water
1/4 tsp. vanilla extract
1/4 tsp. maple flavoring

Combine sugars and water in saucepan. Heat to boiling and boil two minutes; start timing when mixture is bubbling rapidly. Remove from heat; add vanilla and maple flavorings. Store in refrigerator. Serve syrup warm or cold.

Mandarin Sauce

About 1 1/4 cups

3/4 cup unsweetened white grape juice
2 tsp. cornstarch
1 can (10 oz./284 mL) mandarin oranges, drained
1/2 tsp. grated lemon rind
1/8 tsp. cinnamon

Combine grape juice and cornstarch in small saucepan or microwavable bowl; stir. Cook over medium heat or in microwave, stirring frequently until sauce is smooth and thickened. Stir in oranges, lemon rind and cinnamon and cook until heated through. Serve warm over pancakes.

Berry-Apricot Brandy Preserves

There is no need to buy gourmet jams when you can make your own, with your signature and the taste of home-made goodness. This recipe can be made on top of the stove as well as by microwave. The procedure is the same; bring jam to a boil, boil one minute and proceed as for microwave directions.

Makes about 5 cups

5½ cups whole frozen strawberries
4 cups sugar
¼ cup lemon juice
1 pouch liquid pectin
⅔ cup apricot brandy

Thaw berries in a large (three- or four-litre) microwavable bowl on "Defrost" (or 30 to 35 per cent power) until berries can be crushed with a potato masher or pastry blender. (A food processor is too efficient; it liquefies soft fruits.)

Crush most of the berries, leaving some as pieces. Stir in sugar and lemon juice and let stand 10 minutes.

Cover bowl loosely with wax paper; cook on High power for 10 to 12 minutes, stirring twice, until mixture comes to a full rolling boil. Remove cover and boil one minute.

Immediately stir in pectin and apricot brandy. Stir frequently for five minutes and skim off foam. Pour jam into hot, sterilized jars, distributing fruit evenly among jars. Cover at once with two-piece lids or melted paraffin wax.

Recipe Index

T

V

W

Y

Order Form

Please send _____ copies of Savour the Seasons at $15.95 each plus GST ($1.12) plus $2.50 for shipping and handling. Total $________

Payment is by VISA ___ Mastercard ___
Card Number__________________ Expiry Date________________
Or send cheque or money order payable to:

The Kitchener-Waterloo Record,
Attn: Savour the Seasons,
225 Fairway Rd. S.,
Kitchener, Ont., N2G 4E5

Name:____

Address:____

____

Postal Code:____

- -

Order Form

Please send _____ copies of Savour the Seasons at $15.95 each plus GST ($1.12) plus $2.50 for shipping and handling. Total $________

Payment is by VISA ___ Mastercard ___
Card Number__________________ Expiry Date________________
Or send cheque or money order payable to:

The Kitchener-Waterloo Record,
Attn: Savour the Seasons,
225 Fairway Rd. S.,
Kitchener, Ont., N2G 4E5

Name:____

Address:____

____

Postal Code:____